It's About Time You Save Money!

IT'S ABOUT TIME YOU SAVE MONEY!

Olfa Bo

Copyright © Olfa Bo 2024

All rights reserved. No part of this publication may be reproduced, stored in a retrieval system, or transmitted in any form or by any means, electronic, mechanical, photocopying, recording, or otherwise, without written permission of the publisher.

ISBN:

For permission to reproduce excerpts, use copyrighted material, translate, or adapt this work, please contact the auhor or publisher.

Why did I write this book and why do I think you should read it?

Because to me saving money is essential for survival. I like to be in control and knowing I have money in case something happens eases my anxiety of the future. I was raised this way too. I come from a family of 6 living on a single salary, so my parents had to cut costs wherever they could. And why pay a 100 when you can pay half price for the same thing? Having savings gives me comfort and helps me plan my future and reach my goals. I don't want money for the sake of having money but I want to save enough to be comfortable financially and to own at least a house & why not a few more as an investment for my retirement.

Also, I never wanted to be a slave to a job. If I have enough money in the bank, then I can leave a job instead of being miserable at work because I can't afford to. Money can be your pass to freedom and free time.

And to be perfectly honest, I love a bargain.

So, I just wanted to humbly share my findings to help people who struggle to save money. I was one of these people before. I used to spend like there was no tomorrow. Then, I woke up and thought this is not a way of living a life if I want to be comfortable in the future. I need to balance enjoying my life now and saving for my future. So I did and managed to buy a property as an investment with just my savings, no mortgage. It is small, but to me it is just the beginning.

Now, saving money is needed more than ever before. In a lot of countries, inflation is going through the roof so every cent counts and unfortunately, salaries aren't increasing as fast. We are in a society where we are conditioned to buy a lot and more than we need and mostly, to waste in order to buy more.

For example, can you explain why a small sliced bread loaf is more expensive than a big one? If not cheaper, the value for money is better. No one can explain it, but you pay more for less. And because it is cheaper, then you are going to buy the big one, maybe throw away half of it when it goes bad and do it again.

Apart from encouraging waste, I don't know what that is. We need to deconstruct the idea that we need to buy all the things we are currently buying and for what we do need, let's try to find it at the best price available. But what do we need exactly? According to Maslow's hierarchy of needs, there are 5 levels of needs:

1. Physiological Needs: Physiological needs are the basic human needs like wanting food, water, shelter, warmth, clothes and so on.
2. Safety Needs: When the physiological needs are satisfied, the safety needs come next. It's a feeling of safety, protection from elements, order and security.
3. Belongingness and love Needs: Social needs can include need for love, affection, friendship, and belonging to a group.
4. Esteem Needs: These needs have to do with one's image like self esteem, self-respect, self confidence, status, recognition, approval or appreciation. It's a feeling of prestige and self accomplishment.

5. Self-Actualisation Needs: These needs can be the need for self-development, self-actualisation, self-advancement or achieve one's full potential.

To answer our first question, only the first one is absolutely necessary for your survival. Let's say we need the first two, it is still the same. But Life is meant to be lived and not just survived. We as human beings, want to evolve from just surviving. We want to enjoy life, be successful and, in this day and age, enjoying life usually means spending money.

Nowadays, spending money, owning things, and even sometimes showing off, is what we consider "enjoying life" or being successful. How do we measure happiness? Does owning the last Mercedes make you the happiest person in the world? The answer is no. A Rolex would give you the time the same way a £5 watch would. We usually hear "money doesn't buy happiness" and for a person coming from a middle-class background, I always thought it was not true. I always used to say, only rich people can say that. They don't know what it's like to not have money. Whilst I think money does not buy it, because you cannot just buy happiness, it can help tremendously in life.

And how do you get money apart from winning the lottery or coming from a rich background? You work and you save money. You have to make money and save it until it works for you. If you work hard and save money, you can then have spare money to invest until your investment is enough for you to be comfortable.

Money is a tool, not a final destination. Treat it as it is. Save it or spend it if needed, just one thing, always look at the reason why you are spending it.

Spending money in itself is not an issue (in moderation obviously!). What is? The WASTE. When you waste money because you want to 'treat yourself'. We are drawn to buy coffee to go, order food and spend money 24/7 for things you could easily do by yourself or don't need at all.

You waste money as well, when you want to impress people or when you think it will give you a sense of will make you look wealthy. Having a bag that is worth more than 4 months rent on paper is amazing but it doesn't make you a good person or a successful one. I've seen plenty of broke people with Chanel bags in their hands. Impressing people who don't matter shouldn't be your goal in life so you better learn how to save money to use for something good, something great, something for yourself. Happiness and contentment are a state of mind so if you want one, or both, train your brain instead of always thinking that buying anything will make you happier. Get out of this constant need of spending money for instant fixes of happiness. Rewire your brain to think, can I do it any other way?

Spending money is like a drug, the more you spend, the more you will want to spend. It's like an instant pleasure when you buy. You see something, you get excited and you want it. Then, you think you absolutely need it. Next thing you know, buying is the only way to make you happy. You buy it, then what? You are excited for a few days, weeks, even months maybe. Soon enough, except for a few things, you will get bored of it and forget about it. It will sit with the rest of your belongings.

We are in a society where we are conditioned to spend money. We need to own things to exist. So companies spend a lot of money to push you to buy, not only by investing in their product, but in marketing and communication to create a need in you and play with your fear of missing out. Money makes the economy run. In theory, it's great. But what about your economy? You won't change your habits in a day. If you are not used to it, start small. Set a separate account you can't access with a card and start by even transferring £5 per month. Then increase to £10 and keep increasing the amount. Before you know it, you will have saved £1000 in a year and more.

To make sure you are not wasting your money, ask yourself these questions:

Do I spend it on something useful? Can I do it myself? Can I find it cheaper? Do I spend money to impress people? To prove I succeeded in life? Is it worthy?

And think about when you spend the most. Is it when you are sad? Depressed? When you are happy? Your state of mind might influence your relationship with money. We are conditioned to think spending money will make us feel better. It's the same with alcohol, we drink when we are happy, we drink when we have problems or when we are sad to make us feel better. Do you feel better at that moment? Probably yes. Do you feel better when you are sober? Most likely not.

Also, there is what I call the "treat yourself syndrome". You treat yourself when it's Friday, when it's payday, when it's raining, when your heart is broken, when you are on holiday, when you get a new job. Possibilities are infinite ... but not your bank account. Treating yourself is great, making all excuses possible to do so is a different story. Treat yourself to things that really matter to you. And keep the treats as such, because treating yourself 10 times a day isn't a treat anymore. A treat should be once in a while and in moderation.

In a nutshell, don't just spend money just to spend money. Let me give you some useful insights to treat yourself and still save money. Let's get started!

1. If you still live with your parents, save as much as you can!

If you are working and still living with your parents, I advise you to save as much as you can while you still can. Once you will have rent to pay, bills and so on, depending on your salary of course, you won't be able to save as much. You live rent free or maybe give money to help out, you can save big time while doing everything else on the side as long as you're sensible with your money. I wish I listened to my parents when they told me to save and buy an apartment when I was living at theirs. I would have bought quicker and would have probably saved enough for more by now.

Enjoy and make smart investments folks.

2. Plan everything

Planning in advance can be very boring, but in order to save money, you will have to go the extra-mile. You will have to plan everything involving money from your grocery shopping to your holidays. It is not as hard as it looks. If you are not used to planning everything ahead, it might need adjustments in the beginning, but after, you won't even think about it.

What do I mean by planning? In that case, it's more of a combination between planning and research. You will determine in advance what you need and you will start to research it everywhere you can, compare between websites/shops and so on to make a conscious decision that you bought the thing you wanted for the best price.

You have (or I hope you do) a monthly salary that goes in your bank account each month.

Number 1: You have your static expenses: rent or mortgage, bills and taxes. These ones, there is not much you can do except try to find a cheaper provider for electricity, gas, internet. Just consider your salary is what you are paid minus these expenses. It will give you perspective. Being paid £2000 doesn't mean you have £2000 to spend, it means you have for example £1000 to spend.

Number 2: After this, you still have food to pay for, your travel card, shopping, holidays or car expenses and so on. They are expenses you still need but can be reduced.

Number 3: Then, you have what is left to save and treat yourself.

Planning will help you save on things.

Planning will make you save on number 1 but especially on number 2 to be able to reach the maximum for number 3.

Planning is the key to saving. Always buying things at the last minute or without any research will always make you spend more than you would have if you looked days, weeks or months in advance for what you want/need. If you are not prepared or do not know the value of something, how do you expect to find the best price?

Let's take grocery shopping as an example. We all noticed that from one shop to another, depending on the size and the brand, the prices can vary from simple to double. Planning ahead and comparing prices between the shops will help you buy what you want at the cheapest price. Real example: I love the Nescafé Azera Americano instant coffee. It is pretty much the only instant coffee I can drink. Without any discount, it is around £5.49 for 100 grams. I never bought it at that price. At shop A, it is full price. At shop B, it is £3.50. At shop C, I usually find it discounted at £3. And at shop D, it is £2.75. So from shop A to shop D, it is from simple to double. For the exact same product, you could have two for the price of one. I did my research about that product and found out it was cheaper at shop D. As I don't have any close to home, I go once in a while there and buy 2 or 3 boxes. I organise all my grocery shopping this way. I pretty much compared all the prices of what I usually buy and buy and stock in advance. What is true for one product can be different for another one. I tend to buy what I need where I find it the cheapest, even if it means going to 4 or 5 different places every time.

Think of money saving as an investment. Look at the big picture: you save for a better tomorrow and you will hold on tight to your goals in the long run.

3. Set yourself a goal (or goals!)

Unless you are money savvy in the first place, but you wouldn't need to come for advice if you were, you need to save money for a reason. It doesn't really matter what it is, you just have to need a goal. It could be to buy an apartment or a house, to travel, to start your own business or just to buy a car or something you always dreamed of. Ideally, you would prioritise what you need, such as a place to live in. But it's up to you to know what you want first. I personally travelled a lot before starting to save for a flat. When I got my first real job after uni, I was 23. I didn't think much about saving to buy a flat. I really wanted to travel the world. I started small across Europe and North Africa, and little by little, I went further. I used to save money just to have enough cash to be able to do everything I wanted abroad without restrictions.

My aim is life has never been to be rich, but to have enough money to live without restrictions. What restrictions mean to me? Have an apartment or a house to live in, fully paid and another one to rent to have an extra income when I retire. I want to be able to travel when and where I want without thinking, 'Oh wait! I can't afford it'. To be able to reach this goal, I had to change my ways. I noticed the more I wanted to buy a flat, the more I cut all the useless expenses. I used to spend a lot of money on clothes I didn't wear, on things I didn't need, eating out all the time and one day, I thought if I want to move forward to be comfortable later, I need to stop throwing my money out the window.

From time to time, you will think 'what the heck? I don't care anymore', and you will spend money you should be saving. You will be tempted to spend money all the time. Sometimes, you will be stronger than temptation, sometimes you won't. It's perfectly normal, you will have ups and downs on your journey, don't feel bad about yourself. It's like a diet or trying to lose weight: you will follow a routine and sometimes, you will relapse into old habits. Don't worry unless it lasts for too long. You are already doing great by just trying, one step at a time. Start small and go bigger and try to be consistent. Having a goal will help you stay focussed and motivated. You will think twice before spending money on things you don't need. In the beginning, it will be hard, but the closer you will get to achieving your goal, the more you will save money to reach it.

4. Always keep a balance between spending and saving

Wanting to save money doesn't mean you need to become stingy. They are two different things, and I don't want to tell you to save money for just the sake of having money. Money is a way and not a final destination. By not wanting to spend money at all, you might alienate your friends and family. People will avoid you because you don't want to spend money, and being social is partially about spending money. You must spend money for inviting people over, going to the restaurants, the pub or any other activity, buying gifts for birthdays or anniversaries. You are not going to take your money to the grave, so spend it when needed and save it when you can. All this is not about not spending money, or you missed the point, it is about spending smartly. Let's say you saw a flight at £1000 from A to B. If you don't look at other flights with other companies, you might miss out on a better fare. If you go online and do a little research, imagine you find a different flight for £700. Obviously, everyone would book the second flight! Why spend £1000 when you can £700 for the same thing? Here, you still spend money, but you spend as little as possible, and you can either save the extra £300 or use it to treat yourself on holidays. This is how

I proceed; I want something, I look everywhere for it and if I can afford it, I take the best deal. If I don't, then I cut expenses on other things till I am able to. And It worked pretty well so far!

My point is, if you are trying too hard, you will feel guilty every time you spend money on "unnecessary things". Keep the balance by spending money on things you love and get rid of the unnecessary things that don't make you happy. Having spare money to invest on things you love whenever you want or need is the best feeling, and you will get used to it.

If you spent a bit too much at the beginning of the month, then make sure you are money savvy for the remainder and the other way round. You can do it for every other day or week. If you plan a lot of activities in a week, make sure to be careful about spending money the week before and the week after. Instead of going to the pubs every Friday and Saturday, just pick one day. If you know you have your wedding anniversary coming, go out less to save the money for a nice gift and celebration. The list of examples is endless, and I am not going to write them here, but I think you get it by now.

5. Take cash instead of a card/ Always check your bank account

I know it is always more convenient to pay everything by card, even more so now with contactless payments, but using cash instead of a card will help you save money. How? It's psychological. Not actually seeing the money leaving your wallet will make you spend more because "you don't feel it". If I give you £500 in cash to spend at once, trust me, it will be much more difficult for you to spend it than if I have given you a card with £500. It is probably just seeing the money; makes you realise how much you are actually spending. With a card, it is straight from your bank account, so you know you spend money but it is dematerialised. It's all virtual so basically, using your card instead of cash is like living in WestWorld and not in real life. Always keep your card, just in case you need it, but when going out, go to an ATM, and take cash. This way, you can control your spending. Once you have no more cash left, you know you reached your limit and you can go home.

It works for all situations: shopping spree, restaurants, grocery shopping and so on. This way, you won't buy any extra or go over budget and end up broke at the end of the month. Controlling what you spend is the key to saving money.

Another way of controlling how you spend money is checking daily or every other day your bank account. Nowadays, it is very easy to check your balance online with your bank app. Checking your bank account will help you track your expenses and stop spending when you reach your limit. If you have £300 left in your bank account on the 15th of the month, it is more than time to stop spending money. Sometimes, we don't realise how much we spend in a week or a month and the best way to know it, is to check regularly where the money is! After spending a lot of money, I know it can be scary to look at it. I stressed many times about how much I had left but you will get used to it. If you can't do it that often, at least do it once a week. That way, nothing will come as a surprise.

Tracking and controlling your expenses is one more trick to help you reach your goals!

6. #10daysnospendchallenge

At the end of the month, we all sometimes are short on cash. It is a bit harder to save if you end up spending all your money by the end of each month. Your goal is not to end up at zero money, but to have even a little extra in your bank account. In months when I spent a lot more than usual, I practise the 10 days without spending. Basically, I spent zero money unless absolutely necessary until the next payday. It just helps balance the expense you made at the beginning of the month. I use what I have in my cupboards, don't go to restaurants, don't go shopping, nothing, I even bring food everyday to work. I always stock up, so unless you do too, it will be impossible. The goal is not for you to starve to death, so if you have no food left, buy some. Just don't buy food if you still have some at home. Rather than that, learn how to spend no money for a period of time. It is manageable for anyone. To get used to it, you can start with a shorter period, let's say 6 or 7 days. You just stop spending money unless necessary (to go to work or to buy groceries, not takeaways for example) 6 to 10 days before payday. The days will seem to be lasting forever, but you will find pride in doing it. It's like winning a contest against ourselves and our bad habits. We are just money spending addicts trying to make it through the month. Breaking the habit of spending money all the time is a part of the journey to make great savings!

7. Give time and/or money to charity!

I know it might sound weird to give money when trying to save but spending money to help a good cause might just save you from spending money on useless things. Looking around you and people who are less fortunate can help you realise that you can do better with your money. You might understand it is more important to have a roof on your head and savings in case, God forbid, something bad happens then having the last Chanel bag or a sports car instead of savings will be not of much use. Giving money, to a certain extent, will never make you poorer and will make you feel good about yourself. A good deed is always rewarded, and the reward can come in different ways. Spending time volunteering will prevent you from using this time going to the shops or eating in a restaurant for example. If your budget is too tight, hopefully you will have time to give to charity. If you have neither time nor money, at least buy a little something to give to the food bank. You don't have to give a big amount of money; you give what you can and when you can. It can just be £1 a month, it doesn't matter. Believe if you do good, good will go back to you. If you save a good amount in a month, just give back to the universe a little. Eventually, you will have even more back in return.

8. Drop the Friday and/or Payday treat

Let's start with payday. It's crazy how society is conditioning us to buy. We are in a mindset to spend money we don't even have yet. How many times did you tell yourself, let's treat myself, it's payday today or it will be tomorrow, in a week? Companies expect you to spend money on payday. If you pay attention, you receive more communications around the end of the month. Guess why? Because payday is around the corner! They want to remind you that payday is coming so you can spend it as soon as it comes in. So please, stop spending money to treat yourself just because you just had money coming in. It's your money and it's not free money. You worked hard for it.

Treating yourself is not a problem, it's thinking that treating yourself is kind of 'a must' because you just got paid. Unless you really want something and don't have the money to buy it until payday, don't buy a thing you don't really need/crave just because it's payday and you feel like you need to treat yourself on that day. First, I would advise you to treat yourself after all the bills were paid and you added a bit of cash in your savings. Second, as always, be sure you really want it and you are not just spending money to have this instant happiness fix.

Just like payday, Friday is a day when people feel like they have to treat themselves. You had a hard week, and you want to treat yourself to a nice lunch? Fair enough! But remember if you have a goal with the money, the money you spend on that day is lost. It's the little amounts you spend every day, every week and every month that prevent you from saving money. You might think that you are going to feel guilty if you start thinking like that, but as I said many times, and it will never be enough, the point is not to stop enjoying yourself or just surviving. The point is the balance between spending money to treat yourself, go out, travel and so on and saving money. If at the end of the month, you end up with 10 quids in your pocket because you went 3 times a week to dinner, then it's going to be hard for you to save the money you need for whatever your goal is. Friday is the end of the week, but it doesn't mean that you have to treat yourself. It can be but it doesn't have to especially if you are on a tight budget. Spend less but better 😊.

9. Always look at your bank account

I know this one hurts. I find it hard to look at my bank account when I know I spent a lot of money. Looking regularly, if not everyday at your bank account will help you know how much you have left to spend and save. Sometimes, we spend a lot more than we think until we look at our bank accounts. Tracking your money is another key to saving it. In the beginning, if you are not used to doing it already, you will find it hard but when you get used to it, it's very useful. And with this, you will know instantly if you can afford to buy x, y, z in a minute. No need to go into deep maths, you know how much you have and if it's a go or a no go. Remember, if you don't have a saving account or you still need to transfer the money to that account, deduct the amount you want to save from what you have to not accidentally spend what you were supposed to save. The best way is to set up a savings account with money blocked so at least you know you can't use it.

10. Adopt, don't shop!

I know it might be weird to read this, but in this day and age, people still buy animals instead of rescuing one from the shelter. I know animals you can adopt might not be exactly what you are looking for, but you might be just what they need. Adopting instead of shopping will help you do a good deed and save money at the same time. I am sure in the long run, you feel good about it. I am not here to tell you what is good or bad, I am just here to give you tips on how to save money. And I don't say that buying animals is bad, it's just that there is so much more you could do with your money. I am all about the money so save when and where you can please!

11. Ask for gifts for your birthday

It's not the easiest to do I know but it's the most efficient way to kill 2 birds with one stone. You aren't greedy, but practical. We are adults (or I hope you are if you are working and reading this!) so you have pretty much everything that you need. Instead of buying an extra pair of jeans you don't need, maybe you can ask them whether to help you fund a project or buying things you actually really need. How many of you got gifts they never used or not even liked? I am quite sure everyone, including me. I am not telling you to ask people to buy you a Porsche, right? But if it's what you are after, maybe your friends and family can help you find it. A good example is if you are buying a house, you will be skint soon so you could ask your loved ones for fresh towels, small furniture or just money to help you buy what you need. I've been doing it for years with my family now and it's great. They don't have to think about what they are going to buy me and I don't have to pretend I like something I don't and store one more gift I don't need. It is a bit harsh but at least it's honest. What I used to do as well was buy something I wanted and ask them to participate with the amount they wanted. I never asked for anything more than anyone could afford, and neither should you. Don't make people uncomfortable by asking for unrealistic or expensive gifts. Always ask them to donate the amount they want, or buy what they afford even if it's only £5. This way, no one is going to be uncomfortable when the conversation pops up. Not everyone has cash to spare so be mindful of who you are asking and of how much you are asking for!

12. Use your phone provider discounts/ Negotiate you phone contract

It might not be available for everyone and every country, but if you have any type of discounts with your phone provider, check and use them! People don't think about it but it can save you money. I give you a few examples of rewards with my own phone provider: I have free coffees sometimes (and there is one provider that offers free coffees every Tuesday), I sometimes have free meal deals from Tesco and can buy 2 cinema tickets for £7 (instead of around £25). These are just a few examples and it's just a few bits and pieces, but with all the discounts together, even if you can save £30 a month, it will probably at least refund your phone monthly bill. So, if you have them, at least look at what you can use.

Apart from these advantages you may have with your contract, don't be afraid to negotiate the contract towards the end. Usually, they will not offer you a better phone or a better contract by themselves, so you need to ask. And sometimes, even asking is not enough. Again, I am giving you my example: I was paying £30 per month for a 6 gigabits contract with unlimited phone calls/texts. I had it with a Samsung S9. My contract was coming to an end so I asked the customer service if they could offer me a better offer or at least a better phone. They were probably trying their luck, but they said to me that my contract will increase from £30/month to £35 and I could get a phone but what they offered me wasn't really interesting. I said that it wasn't interesting at all, but the customer service agent said it was the best he could do. I knew I could get much better for much cheaper and as I didn't really need to upgrade to a new phone anyway, I was happy to stay with a sim only contract. Next thing I did was fill the form online to have the code they need to give you when to keep your number and go to the competition. I was ready to leave and then it started, another customer service agent called me a few times to know what happened and why I was leaving. I explained the situation and instead of increasing my bill, I got a £5 discount per month for more data that I could use, and I got a free phone. Of course, it isn't an iPhone 15, but it's more than I need as I am not into buying expensive phones anyway. Always remember to negotiate if you want to stay or check if there is a better deal out there. Don't overpay for something just because you are lazy checking others offers or too shy to negotiate. No one will do it for you, so get to work!

13. Stop thinking because it's cheap, it's fine

Remember the time when you were in the shops, at a coffee place or anywhere else and you were thinking 'oh it's just £3 or £4, it's nothing'? Well, this £3 or £4 will add up to the other 10 times you thought the same this week and the other weeks, I let you do the math. Again, it is not about not buying anything but just stop and ask yourself a few questions:

- Do I need it? For example, do you need to buy a coffee before going home by yourself where you can have coffee? Or is it worth buying a £5 coffee before going to work where you have free coffee? Do I need one more cute notebook when I already have dozens I don't even use? Do I need to buy more cupboard food when I already have so much already?
- Is it worth it? A couple of quids is cheap, but for some things, cheap equals bad quality. If you end up buying 10 times the same thing because it's cheap, is it really that cheap in the end?
- Is there a better/cheaper alternative somewhere? I took a habit of always Googling things I buy to see if they are worth it. Not everything is, but you will find out sometimes that even something

that is as cheap as £4, can be 1 or 2 in a different shop.

These small amounts will make you wonder 'where did all my money go?' So prevent yourself from asking this question by stopping treating small amounts like they don't matter.

14. Save water!

I am saying stating the obvious but SAVE water for your wallet and the planet! If your water bill is through the roof, then read carefully. Simple but useful tips to save water:

- Stop taking baths: you can have some occasionally but stick to once a month or once a week if you really are an addict. A shower does the same job for less water.
- Turn off the taps whenever you are cleaning the dishes, brushing your teeth, soaping your body in the shower. The water doesn't need to run all the time.
- Don't shower for 45 minutes. We all love standing under the hot water, but it won't make you any cleaner. I am sure you can be clean in 15 minutes.
- Drink tap water as it is edible in a lot of places. You will save money and save the planet from plastic.
- If you have stale water, don't throw it away. Reuse it to brush your teeth, water your plants, or wash your floor. It doesn't matter what you do with it as long as you reuse it.

To make it simple and easy: DON'T WASTE WATER.

15. DIY instead of BUY

You might think 'do it yourself' isn't cheaper than buying and it might be true for a few things. But I can say, for most, it is much cheaper to do it yourself than to pay someone else to do it for you. For food, how much can you get for the same price if you cook the same meal vs buying it at the restaurant or at a takeaway place? I'd say around 3 to 4 times more. Not only for food, but instead of buying new furniture, why not upcycle yours? Or maybe upcycle yours and sell them to get the new ones you want? Or buy a second hand one and shape, colour them the way you want? Same for deliveries, it is cheaper to get things yourself than to pay for a delivery.

    I am really not a handywoman myself, but some things are really easy to do. Plus, you will feel a better satisfaction and a sense of accomplishment doing things yourself rather than buying them. You might discover a new passion; it will take your brain out of your daily routine and it can be good for your mental and physical health. We all (or most) work hard and doing minor repairs, painting or building things can be very soothing. And when you're done, the satisfaction and pride you feel is unbuyable.

It doesn't matter what it is you try to do yourself instead of buying, just get into this mindset first that you can do it. We are lucky to be in an era where a phone and internet can give you access to plenty of explanations, tutorials, product comparison so use them. Who knows, maybe you will thank me one day for helping you find your new passion or your new business (and income!) by trying something you couldn't be bothered or thought you couldn't do.

16. Always subscribe to newsletters

No one likes to be spammed, no one! But hey, little tip from the insider, most people who subscribe to newsletters get special offers you don't. It will depend on the brand, but a lot of brands in retail give you X percent off just by signing up. As it can be overwhelming, I advise you to do it for the brands you really want to buy something from, subscribe a couple of days or weeks and look at their emails, app notifications or SMS to see if they give you a special offer. This goes back to what I said previously, if you want to buy anything, always plan and look around. Buying at the best price requires organisation, so get yourself together. And if you don't mind receiving a lot of emails, then subscribe to all the brands you like. That way, you always know what to expect and what offer you can have when you are ready to buy. Some brands will offer you an 'entry discount' and maybe even more if you don't buy straight away. Remember, their goals are to make you buy so they are going to try different techniques. One might be to give you money off of your first item if 10% off didn't work. Same goes for inactive customers, they will try to bring you back by offering you discounts.

And on a side note, don't expect luxury brands to give you even 1% off on an email. No, they just don't do it. So, if you sign up to a newsletter for a Chanel bag or a Ferrari, not gonna happen. I mean, I don't know if you can negotiate a Ferrari price but, no, they don't give 10% off of their cars by email or SMS. They might give me a free ride, but that's about it.

17. Ask yourself, why do I need to buy this?

I used to be the queen of buying things I didn't need so I will tell you that from experience, asking yourself this question could save enough to buy a brand new car (not quite a Lamborghini, but one can dream!). I am not talking about a need, but about the extra. It's like going to the supermarket when you are hungry: you are 100% gonna buy more than planned and crave a lot of food you will not eat in the end. It doesn't mean that you will not eat them at all, but when hungry, you fancy a lot that ends up not being that interesting when you are full. This happens with compulsive shopping. You see it, you want it and then the excitement goes away and you forget about it. And on to the next.

Secondly, we buy things we don't need to impress people or to feel better about ourselves. Both are somehow wrong: you can't buy happiness. Yes, it's better to cry in a Mercedes than in a Vauxhall or in your penthouse, but that's not the topic. I am talking about buying things to make you feel better because you are sad, depressed, lonely, ... It might make you feel better for a second, but this feeling will go away as fast as it came. Instead of buying to fill the void you have in yourself, try to fix why you feel this void. I am no therapist, and I won't pretend I can give you life advice, but try to talk to someone instead of buying your pain away. It's like drinking to forget the pain, it always comes back the next day.

If you buy to impress, then sorry to disappoint, but no one cares. First, you are fooling no one. Especially people that know you. Everybody knows that some people can't afford to eat but spend all their money on expensive clothes, cars, and going out to the best restaurants to show off. And for people who don't know you, why try to impress them? They don't know you, they don't care and so should you. Who are you trying to impress? Who are you trying to prove yourself to? What are you trying to prove? There is no shame in wearing cheap clothes and driving an affordable car. It doesn't mean you are not successful in your own way. We all look at people travelling in first class, with luxury cars and houses and we feel like we have nothing, or worse, like WE ARE nothing. Again, I am not a therapist but just a little advice: money doesn't grow on trees, life is easy on some people and hard on others. Some people were born rich, good for them. Others worked hard and became rich and good for them. More worked hard their entire life and never became rich. It doesn't make them bad, it doesn't make them miserable or it doesn't mean they are not good enough or successful in their own way. Success is not measured by the amount of money you have or pretend you have. We all have different life aspirations, and we all have different things to deal with in life. No one has the same cards to play with at the poker of life so stop trying to compare yourself and to impress people. I know the saying 'fake it till you make it'. Faking it is not going to make you succeed. I am a sucker for inspirational posts on Instagram buuuuuuuuuuuuuuuuut, yeah it is a big but, it created an ideal life (99% fake), the need to pretend our life is perfect and make people feel guilty 'when they didn't make it'. If you are not rich today, it's because you didn't do X,Y,Z. No life is perfect, and no, not because you aren't rich doesn't mean you failed, or you didn't work hard. Find your own path, build solid foundations and hopefully, you will succeed. Your success might just be to buy a little house, to be a housewife/husband, to own a local business. It doesn't matter, but the minute you spend all your money to try to impress others, it's the first minute of a lot you are adding to the amount of time you are from reaching your financial/personal goal. So quit the 'fake it till you make it' and save the money to actually MAKE IT. And by the way, if you've never noticed I am telling you, people who are the richest never try to show off to anyone.

18. Shop in shops vs shop online

I noticed many times before that online deals are better than shop deals, especially in retail. It might not be true for every brand, but a quick Google can help you. I might not save the high street with this one, but I am here to give you tricks on how to save money and get better deals. Online, you can have sales you don't have in stores, special deals, more choice and sometimes 10% or more off depending on the brand. So before buying in a shop, have a quick look online to check if you can get a better deal. Obviously, it is not an invitation to buy more as it can be more tempting online. Remember, the more dematerialised it is, the less you are likely to 'feel' the purchase and the value of what you buy. Psychologically, it was harder to let out cash than to spend it with a card/online. Hence why now we can buy a lot more with cards than ever before (and for other reasons but that's a different story). So, don't scroll too much and buy what you want and that's it. Online shopping has so much choice that we could literally blow up a month's salary at payday. And before buying a thing online, check the delivery cost and return policy. If you end up paying high shipping and return fees, there is no point. If you buy online and don't like the item but you have to pay to send it back, it might not be worth it as well.

Or worse, you could miss the return window and end up with something you are never going to wear. Shop smartly is always key. And a good wifi connection is ... well very useful sometimes.

19. Buy promotions!

I know it might sound weird to say it but take full advantage of discounts in stores. It doesn't matter if it is half price, buy one get one free, or any type of promotion, it will make you save a few bucks. Be careful, I said PROMOTIONS, not buying in packs. They are two different things and buying in packs doesn't necessarily mean you will save money. Sometimes you can save money, but usually less than £1 for food and in some cases, I noted that buying a pack of 3 biscuit boxes was more expensive than buying them separately. In that case, why buy a pack if it works out more expensive than buying only one? It is not always the case, but I always advise you to check the price of packs against the price of one item to see if there are savings to make. Going back to promotions, they are things you need to keep in mind: only buy things you will really use or like. Sometimes, we just buy things we think we will eat or use, and they end up in the bin because we don't. So only focus on items you like or will actually use. Second, be really careful with fresh food promotions. Usually, the best before date is close, hence the promotion. It is not always the case, but keep in mind to check the dates and be sure to eat it while it's still edible. If the date is far, make sure to not forget it in a cupboard or in the fridge.

If you have favourite products, always check if there are no promotions on them before buying as promotions can sometimes be in the middle of the store or on a different shelf. With time, you will know what always comes back on offer so you will be able to wait a bit more to have the same thing at half price!

Buying things on promotion is great for saving money, but not so great if the food ends up in the bin. You will in the end spend more money and waste food at the same time so make sure you will eat what you buy!

20. Use food waste apps!

There is a saying "one man's trash is another man's treasure". It has never been so true! People become more conscious about the environment and waste. There are plenty of anti-waste apps in the market and in all countries and if there is none in your country, maybe it's an idea you could develop. In the UK, there is Olio, it's a free app where you can post food and non-food items, and request to collect. So if you are going on holiday and don't want to waste what's on your fridge, this app is fantastic. They have food waste heroes too who collect food from Tesco, Pret a Manger or other brands and list them for free for people to collect. If you are on a budget, this can be a good way to save money and avoid waste. I used it before, and I saved a lot on meals. I even discovered food I would never think of buying by myself for various reasons. Whether you post or you collect, you will win. If you post, then you save food from waste and do a good deed and if you collect, then you save food from waste and save a few bucks on the way.

There are other apps like 'too good to go' where shops sell a basket full of food for a certain price. The difference obviously is you have to pay for the food but usually, prices are at least 50% off. Depending on the shops, the offers are more or less interesting. Plus, bear in mind you can't really choose what will be in your basket, so it's better to be something you like in the first place. Bonus point if you bought from there before, at least you will know what to expect.

I just listed two apps I know of, but there are plenty in the market, offering different options. Use the ones that will suit you the most and you will be able to make great savings while helping stop the waste of food! Not all superheroes wear caps 😊.

21. Think (former) hard discount

When I was younger, Aldi, Lidl and other hard discounters didn't have a very good reputation. It was cheap, for sure, but the quality was too, or so we thought. Well, I have good news for you: They aren't anymore! If you are attached to specific brands, I don't say that their own brand can replace them, but for a lot of things it can. If you haven't seen the videos of Americans going to Lidl for the time, please go and Google it now, it's so worth it. They were like kids in a Disney store, full of aww when they saw fresh pastries and cheap products all the way through. There are some really good quality products for a very good price, you might be surprised at how cheap things are. The vegetables are overall good, you can even find organic, vegan or free from food for half of the price. You don't need to buy everything from there, unless you want to, but you can mix your grocery shopping between shops. You can buy your essentials from there like pasta, rice and what you can buy from there or don't like, buy it somewhere else. We pretty much buy the same things all the time, so with a bit of practice, you will know what to buy where. I do it all the time, I navigate between shops, usually not on the same day. I will make a stock of long-lasting food and buy weekly fresh food to avoid waste. I just gave you two names as they are the only ones I know but I am sure there are plenty of them all over the world. Just find your local one and enjoy shopping for cheap!

23. Buy short dated food / destroyed packaging / buy ugly vegetables

In most shops, you can find on the side items "reduced to clear" with a new barcode and much cheaper than usual. They usually have a best before date ending soon (the day itself, and no more than 2 days I'd say) or a damaged packaging.

A destroyed packaging won't affect use for many products, like sanitary towels for example. You can buy the same thing for a fraction of the price just because there is a little damage. If it's food, make sure it is still fresh. If you buy a damaged biscuit box, even if they are covered with plastic, they can have this old taste, so avoid it. To be able to save when buying damaged packaging, make sure it won't affect use, that it is the same as buying an undamaged one, that nothing is missing, and you will be fine.

On the side of supermarket alleys, you can find short dated food to buy at a discounted price. The discount can be from 50 to 99% depending on when the best before date is. It is a very good way to save money on fresh food, pastries and bakery, but in order to save and not waste money, you need to think about how you are going to use what you buy. Are you going to eat everything before it becomes inedible? Can you freeze it? Are you going to eat it or are you just buying it because it's cheap? If you reply yes to at least two of the three then you are good to go.

Finally, you can now find "ugly fruits or vegetables" in supermarkets. Fruits and veggies are calibrated so when they were out of shape, farmers used to throw them away. If you don't mind having a wonky courgette or carrot, and you care more about the taste than the looks, you can definitely try to look out for those. They are cheaper for the exact same taste just because people want good looking food! The prices vary from one shop to another, but I am quite sure you can save from 25 to 50% of the price.

Saving money is also about trying to look everywhere for a bargain, so open your eyes when you shop!

24. Always use what is in your fridge or cupboards first!

It might sound obvious, but it's not. Most of the time, we buy new things instead of using what we have in the fridge or cupboards. It might be because we don't fancy what we already have, because it's easier than digging into your piles of food, or because we forget what is in there. I am sure there are plenty of reasons why we buy food we sometimes already have. I have the problem of forgetting what I have in my cupboards or falling for promotions when I see some. I ended up having way too much long-lasting food like pasta and so on. While I am sure I will eat them at some point, I started hating pile up food which most of the time I wasn't able to remember I had. I took the habit of stopping buying food I am craving at the end of the month and using what I had. I also try now to organise my cupboards by freshness. I put in the front, what is going to expire first. I then use it even when I am not craving it, especially at the end of the month when I wait for the next payday. It took me a long time to do it and sometimes, I would find that something I finally decided to use, the best before date has expired. I hate waste in general, and I hate food waste even more as I am lucky enough to have more than I should when some people are starving. Learning how to use what is left before buying anything will make you not only save but stop wasting money. As we have a lot of choices in shops, takeaways or now delivery everywhere, I know it can be hard to prioritise using what you already have, especially when you crave it. I suggest you simply don't go to the supermarket until you really need to. If you absolutely have to, then avoid aisles where you could buy what you already have or what you don't need at that moment. It might sound contradictory to what I said before about buying stocks when things are in promotions, but it isn't. You don't need to buy every time you see a promotion. You need to buy a stock while the price is interesting and then use what you bought until you finish it and then you can buy again. If you are close to finishing it and find another good promotion, go for it, otherwise leave it.

25. Try to be vegetarian few times a week

If you are not already vegetarian, you might not like that one, especially if you are a meat lover. Meat is good, but it is the most expensive food as well, especially if you want good quality. Eating meat with every meal will triple your grocery budget if not more. Vegetarian meals you cook yourself can be worth less than £1! Meat is not recommended on a daily basis and not on every meal. The excess of meat can be bad for our health and bringing a bit of variety in life never hurt anyone. If you try to eat meat every other day, twice or three times a week, your body and your wallet will thank you. If you are not a veggie lover, just learn tricks to find vegetables more appetising. Invest in stocks, caramelised onions, crispy onions, nuts, herbs and spices on top of the classic onions and garlic and I promise you will enjoy eating meat free meals. It could be an opportunity for you to try new recipes and to be creative when cooking. You could create your own tasty sauces to mix with vegetables (you could do that with meat too, but here, I am trying to convince you to eat less meat ok!). We all had once in our life the "What I am going to cook today?" Well, when you have plenty of vegetables, you have plenty of options. With google, blogs, Instagram and so on, it is really easy to find recipes, so you have no excuse! If it is too hard for you to not eat meat at all, try to do the opposite. You can start by eating veggie meals two or three times a week, get used to eating plant-based food and then little by little, replace most of your meaty meals with veggie meals. I became flexitarian a few years ago, and all I can say is now, I enjoy eating meat more than before. Eating meat everyday made it so normal, I wasn't enjoying it anymore. Now, I appreciate the taste more than before and enjoy having good meat on the menu.

If you really don't want to stop eating meat, eat less red meat and replace it with white meat. It is much cheaper so you can get more for your money.

26. Don't buy ready meals / meal kits

Yes, they are nice, yes you are tired when you go back from work, but NOOOOOO don't buy them. It doesn't matter how tempting they are, you could have the same for half, if not less than this price. Plus, it's not good for your health. Ready meals are full of sugar, salt, fat and other things to make it yummier, and we all know it's the perfect combo to gain weight without realising. If you fancy any of them, buy the ingredients and try to make your own at home, you will save money and calories at the same time! I know it takes more time, but at least for the price of one ready meal, you will be able to feed your entire family or batch cook for yourself. Keep the rest in your fridge or freezer. At least, you will know what's in your food and even if it's not a perfectly balanced meal, it will always be better if you do it yourself. We are allowed to have cheat meals sometimes (or all the time, but that depends on you), so you do you!

It works the same for meal kits, they are nice and are supposed to save you time (or avoid you ruining a meal), but in the end, you still cook, it's more expensive than buying ingredients separately and again, you don't control the amount of salt, sugar and fat they add in. I will give you an example of katsu curry. I thought it was a really hard meal to make, don't ask me why, so I bought a kit because I love it and wanted to try it at home. Well, I did it and it was good but after that, I found a recipe explaining how to do it. I thought I'd give it a try and well, mine was better and much cheaper. For the amount I did myself, I made 4 meals versus only 2 for the meal kit. It takes a little more time, obviously, but I was controlling everything, especially as I don't like salt in my food.

One last is food boxes with veggies, meat and recipes. I never tried it myself, but I find it quite pricey. You buy a box full of ingredients which would cost you a fraction of the price and you have recipes you can find everywhere. But if it suits you and avoids wasting food, then go for it. For it to work, you have to only use the ingredients in the box for your meals, otherwise in my opinion, you defeat the purpose. I cook with my cravings so it would never work for me, as I don't know what I will want in advance, but I am wondering, what if you don't like one of the boxes or recipes? I prefer to choose what I cook but I understand people want to avoid the hassle of finding a meal to cook and having to buy groceries. Just do it if it suits you and your lifestyle and make sure you don't waste. It's my only advice.

Give yourself credit, you can do it yourself! And even if you ruin the recipe, at least you tried. If you succeed, then great. You got this.

27. Be aware of marketing techniques

Some brands, in order to make more money and to have better deals with major supermarkets, will produce the same product for them and for the supermarkets. The first one will be labelled with the brand and the second one will be labelled under the supermarket brands. It is the same content, but not the same packaging and definitely not the same price. The supermarket one could be half the price of the branded one, if not more sometimes. I can't give you a discount range as it can vary from one product to another. As an example, L'Oréal, the famous French cosmetic company sold their shampoo in Carrefour, a French supermarket under their brand, and sold the same shampoo to Carrefour for their own brand. It was exactly the same with a little difference: the l'Oréal one was 3 or 4 times more expensive. Same for the Lipton Ice Tea. It was identical to the supermarket brand one. This is why sometimes; you find that supermarket brands have a very similar taste to the branded ones. It doesn't work for everything and it is very hard to prove as they will keep it a secret, but if the taste is the same, buy supermarket labels, you might end up with the same for cheaper. If it's not exactly the same but you like the taste, who cares if there is no brand. The only thing that matters is saving money when you can. We did a blind test with Iced tea in a marketing class with people who claimed there was a difference between the branded and non-branded one. Well, all I can say is without the bottle, they couldn't tell which one was which.

Another technique to make you buy more and more expensive products is to put them at your level or put them in the centre. Supermarkets will put the cheaper option on the lowest or highest shelves so the first you will see is the one they want you to buy. If you are a bargain chaser like me, it won't work for you but, for people who don't pay attention, they will buy the first one they see. Just have a quick look up and down before making your selection.

Now that you are aware, keep your eyes peeled!

28. Couponing/loyalty programs

They are two different things but both can save you money. I put them together as some loyalty cards might work along coupons. Whether it's coupons or a loyalty program, just have a look at it and see if it's worth it. Some of them are, some of them are not.

Coupons can save a lot of money. Have a look at where, when, and how you can get them. Usually, they are given to you when you buy specific products or just buy from a shop. They can be put in your mailbox as well, to push you to buy. It doesn't matter how you get them, as it may vary a lot from one place to the other. Just make sure they actually make you save money and not buy unnecessary products that will end up in the bin!

Loyalty programs/cards can take many forms depending on the brand: Private sales for members, accumulating points till you get freebies or buy an item with the points (or pay with points and add money if necessary, like they do in most airlines), a percentage or money off every purchase, coupons to buy at a reduced price and so on. I can't list them all as I am sure I don't know a quarter of them. Most of them are free so why not give them a chance?

Just remember something, the goal is to save money so again, only use these coupons/loyalty cards if they are really going to make you save money, not something you didn't want in the first place because it is cheap/with a discount.

29. If the shops are not too far, walk!

I know it's more convenient, but unless you need to shop for a lot of people, you usually don't need a car to carry everything (unless you buy heavy products). Most of the time, we buy more than we should because we will put everything in the car, and we won't have to carry them. If you go to the supermarket with a trolley, trust me you will buy only what's necessary as you don't want to have to carry more on the way back. Plus, you save money on petrol and petrol isn't cheap these days!

It's also good for you and for the environment. Getting fresh air and walking is good for your brain and easy exercise. I don't tell you to walk 3 hours in the snow, rain, or extreme heat, but if it is half an hour away and you can, why not walk? A save is a save, it doesn't matter how much you will save in the process. Every pence will add on and you would be surprised how much you can get from just saving a few quids here and there.

Buying groceries is a big part of our lives and spendings, so choose wisely. Supermarkets are here to make you buy more, even if it means wasting food in the end. Smaller sizes are most of the time more expensive than the same one in a bigger size? Or the price difference is so small that you end up buying the biggest one for getting a better value for your money. It's all made to make you spend more and waste. And then, you buy again and again and again, it's an endless cycle. Before you know it, your cupboards are full, but yet you keep buying new things because this is how we are trained to be. We need to have our cupboards full to feel like we have enough food. We love abundance. You stock and you forget what is in the back till the expiry date arrives or long due.

30. Eat your breakfast at home!

I know it might sound weird for some people and it's probably cultural, but when I moved to the UK, I noticed that a lot of people were eating their breakfast at work or grabbing something on the way to work. Coming from France, it was very rare to see people eating their breakfast at work, and it was mostly people who were trying to save time in the morning. If you have a free breakfast at work, knock yourself out. Usually, free breakfasts at work are good and overall healthy. I am the type of person who needs a coffee at home to wake up, but I don't judge. But if you have to pay for it, at your workplace or on your way to work, then don't. How much does a coffee cost? How much is going to cost your fruit salad and anything that will go nice with it? Probably at least a fiver, and most likely £8 to £10 or maybe more. So, if I take the cheapest option, £5, you will pay £25 a week just for breakfast. And this is the cheapest option! It makes it around £100 a month just to eat your breakfast. It is at least a week worth of groceries for 2 people (maybe more). It doesn't seem to be a lot when you buy it and you are probably thinking 'oh, it's just a few quids' but the few quids you are dropping everyday is the reason why you are broke at the end of the month. Saving money is learning how to drop this bad habit of spending money on little things that pile up and end up being a lot. If you have to pay £1200 for something, you will give it a thought before spending all that money. So why spend hundreds a month without a second thought? Keep your outdoors breakfast as a treat, when you have quality time with your friends or when you really are late for work. Trust me, your wallet will thank you later.

31. Stop buying coffees all day, every day!

Same as breakfast, stop buying coffees outside every single day. I am a coffee lover, so trust me, I know what is the joy of buying one. But hey, good news, there is an awesome thing called coffee machine. You can buy one and a have good quality coffee at home. Plus, if you are a bargain hunter like me, you could buy really good quality coffee for next to nothing. Not so long ago, I bought organic coffee from Holland&Barrett reduced at a bargain price of 33p. So, yes coffee in a coffee shop is great but it is expensive on a daily basis.

If you have free coffee at work, use it instead of going out to buy one. If you don't, why not invest with your colleagues on a coffee machine and divide the costs (unless you are planning to leave soon, obviously!). If you can have coupons for free coffee, use them. For example, Vodafone offers free coffees every now and again. Same as breakfasts outside, keep the coffee as a treat. You will save lots with a little effort. If you really think you can't do it, at least bring your reusable cup, most coffee shops give you a discount if you do. And it's good for the planet. This time, your wallet and the planet will thank you.

32. Batch cooking fellas

It's boring and long, I know. But once it's done, it will save you TIME and MONEY, two of my favourite things in the world! I am quite sure you are asking yourself 'how would it help me save money?', well guess what? You are right, it doesn't! Obviously, I am only joking. How? Simple maths: if you cook in batches, then you need to be organised. Organisation is planning your meals in advance and going shopping with a list of ingredients you need. Plus buying in bulk or in bigger quantities is usually cheaper. You also have the offers to buy one get one free, the second for half the price that could help. No extra spending, no waste! If you stick to your plan and don't order food after eating twice the same meal, you will save some money. If you do, then freeze the food for when you are too lazy to cook and tempted to order in. And why not use the extra time to work on building your business, crafting, selling clothes or anything you no longer use, learn a new skill? Anything to help you get more money in the short or long run.

33. Bring your own food at work

A consequence of batch cooking is you have a lot of food in your fridge/freezer. Instead of buying food at lunch when you go to work, take what's in your fridge. Unless you have free food at work obviously, and you would be very lucky, but that goes without saying. If you are too lazy to really cook, you still have tons of alternatives. You could prepare a big salad at home (and it's a very healthy option too), you could use your dinner leftovers, you could have instant noodles, canned soup, anything but buying food at lunch. A lot of recipes take less than 30 minutes to prepare so even the laziest person can do it. When you buy food at lunch, you are hungry (obviously) and will have all sorts of cravings. The outcome of cravings is spending a lot of money to stop your mouth from watering. Even if £7 or £15 don't sound like 'a lot', in fact it is. If you buy a lunch at £10 every now and then because you fancy it, it's fine, but if you do it every day, then it all adds up. For an average of £10 per day, you will end up spending £50 per week just for food for your lunch. And let's be honest, when you buy food at lunch, you rarely spend less than £10, most likely more than that for a good meal. This will be your budget for all your meals for a week. My advice is, bring your homemade meals at work to eat at lunch and save buying food from outside as a treat or as a last option if you didn't have time to cook or bring something. Keep it as a Friday treat, or as a treat when you feel low and you feel like food will cheer you up (yes, for me food is life). Saving is cutting useless expenses and sorry, but buying lunch is one of them. It might be a bit difficult to commit to it in the beginning but saving hundreds a month should motivate you!

34. Take a look at your commute to work...

Are you taking public transportation or your own car?

If you are taking public transportation, make sure you are on the best plan possible. It means having a look at what you are spending and if you have cheaper options/ way of saving money. I bet you are asking yourself how? I give you a quick example, in London, you have yearly, monthly, weekly plans and pay as you go. You also have a plan for buses, only others for trains, metro and so on. If you travel only 5 days a week taking only the tube, it is cheaper to use pay as you go. If you use different types of transportation 5 days a week, it is more interesting to take a weekly card and most likely a monthly or yearly card (monthly and yearly cards are most likely cheaper but the weekly one was set up as an example). But if you do travel 3 days a week, then you are better off staying in a pay as you go plan. Taking buses only to commute? Buses are half the price, so go for it. It might be cheaper for you to pay a few extras when you need something else. Most companies offer a scheme where they pay the yearly pass for you and deduct it from your pay. Just remember, before asking for it, ask yourself if you are going to fully use it. If not, then save the money for something else. Depending on where you live, the prices obviously differ, and I can't tell you for sure what will be interesting for you. Have a look at all the options for a month, compare and make your decision. You can always adjust your plan later if your needs change.

If you are taking your car, have you ever thought about taking public transport? Sometimes, it is easier and less hassle. For a 45 min drive vs a 45 min in public transports, you save a lot of money on petrol and you can read a book, play games, release the stress from work. Plus, you might be able to find car insurance that makes you pay based on kms you actually do, and you could save on that side too. And remember, less kms, less maintenance. I know it will largely depend on where you live, where you work or if you have to drop off your kids before and after school or run errands. Just a little note to check if you can qualify for a company car. Usually, when you start working somewhere, they will tell you, but sometimes this perk is set aside and forgotten (not on purpose of course lol), especially when you get promoted. If you want to stick to the car, have you ever thought about carpooling? It doesn't have to be with a colleague, but it could be with someone around. This is a good way to save money and who knows, make new friends! Or do you ever compare gas station prices? From one to the other, you can save a lot too. I don't say drive for miles to find a cheap one because you would defeat the purpose, but if you find a few on your way, just check and remember prices. Once you know which one is the cheapest, always choose this one to fill up your tank.

Also, there are apps where you can rent your car when you don't need it. If you need the money, why not look at this option too?

One more and I will stop with this one as I feel it's touching a nerve, have you ever thought about cycling or walking to work? I know it's not doable for everyone, I myself can't walk to work and I am scared to death of biking cycling in the city. But if you are braver than me, cycling could be a good option. If you are not used to cycling during rush hours, please practise before and invest in proper protection gears! It's cheap and good for your health. Walking will depend on how far you live from work, but if it's a 40 min maximum, it would be worth giving it a shot. Walking is FREE and good for your physical and mental health. I love walking, you see so much you wouldn't see in a car, in public transportation or on a bike.

Now get to work and find the best and cheapest option to commute!

35. Plan your wedding a long time in advance ... if possible

Planning is key to saving money and I am pretty sure I said it several times. Well, it's true for weddings as well. Unless you didn't plan to get married and rushed it, plan everything a long time in advance so you can have a look at all the options for wedding venues, DJs, caterers, dress, cake and so on and to be sure to choose the best bargains for everything. It doesn't mean you need to take the cheapest options, but it will allow you to have time to maybe find a good venue, cake or DJ for half the price as other ones for the same service or quality. Be sure to select plenty of options and make a decision based on your wishes and within your budget.

Secondly, Having a budget is important, especially for weddings. We all get excited and want doves and fireworks, but if you don't have a budget and stick to it, you will end up spending much more than you wanted to in the first place, and even much more than what you can afford. Budget accordingly and stick to it.

Thirdly, have a to do list and for each 'to do point', write the budget you have for it. Once you know how much you are going to pay for each one, write it down so at a glance, you know how much your budget was and how much you spent. This way, if you spent less than planned then you have more room for unexpected last minute spends or, add it to your honeymoon fund and enjoy yourself.

36. Think preloved or sample sales for your wedding

We all dream of the perfect suit ... and mostly the perfect dress. We always drool over the designer dresses that cost a fortune. But, just remember, your wedding is going to last a day so your wedding dress will only be worn for ... a day. Spending a fortune on a dress is what people regret the most after their wedding. First because wedding dresses don't hold their value. It doesn't matter if you bought it for £5000, wore it just once (well we hope) and dried it clean, you'd be lucky to have half of it back. Plus, as stated before, you will only wear it for one day and it will remain stored in your place until you decide to dispose of it. You have some nice, yet cheaper alternatives to say yes to the dress.

The preloved market might not be the best for sellers, but it's a different story on the buyers' side. You might find your dream dress at a much better price. People like to think the bride wants to keep her dress and it's true but it will half the place in the wardrobe. People might keep it for emotional reasons, but in the end most sell it or give it away. So, this is your chance! There are plenty of websites, social networks groups and pages where you might be able to find the dress of your dream at a fraction of the price. I know it's not nice to lean on others' despair but hey, we are here to save money.

Another trick for wedding dresses/suits is to look for brides'/grooms' shops and wait for the sales or buy a sample sale item. If you aren't in a rush, again you could end up buying what you want with a fair discount.

A wedding is already expensive as it is, so if you can save a bit, you shouldn't think twice. Preloved or sales items are as lovely as buying brand new (most of the time) so dig a bit and do a bit of research before buying new.

If you can afford it, buy new. But well, buying new won't help you save money. And that is the main goal of this book.

Last but not least, don't forget after your wedding to sell your dress, you won't make a lot back but it's still money you can reuse for something else. Take your time if you feel like you can't, as it can't be hard to let go of the memory of your amazing day. But eventually, I am pretty sure you will. Remember, wedding dresses run out of style so if you are willing to sell, don't wait too long.

36. Think DIY

Yes, weddings are expensive. I am repeating myself, but it's just to convince you that you can still have the wedding of your dreams and manage to save money or at least spend less than expected.

Before buying very expensive decorations or getting a wedding planner, look at what you can do yourself. Bits and pieces can be done by yourself and can save you a lot. Like the centrepieces, you can easily decorate it yourself with a bit of imagination or just by looking for ideas online. There is a lot that can be done to save money so make a list of all your needs, the extras you might have and define your budget. When you are done, first, put aside what you can't do by yourself then compare how much it will cost you to do things yourself and to pay for them. If you have a reasonable amount that you can do by yourself and save money, then do it. I say reasonable because remember, weddings can be very stressful, so you don't want to set high expectations and fail at the last minute because you don't have time. Or worse, end up being constantly stressed and depressed because you have too many things to do. Weddings are supposed to be a happy day, so keep things easy, and don't stress yourself. When you have a ready list of your DIY, keep track of your progress to avoid missing a thing.

37. When possible, create a wedding list or ask for money as a gift

I know it's not always easy to ask for money, but no one ever shows empty handed to a wedding so try to make the best of it. We all know weddings are expensive so why not create a money pool for people to put the amount of money they want to help you fund your wedding and/or honeymoon. Not everyone can afford to spend a lot of money for gifts so at least, they will give you what they can and for you, it will add up to the rest and help you cover the costs. The problem is with gifts you haven't asked for, they can be useless to you for various reasons. If you have your home full of everything, you don't need one more dinner set, do you? It might not be according to your liking as well then what do you do with it? Resell it? It can be a sensitive topic, so just specify that if they want to, they can. No pressure and you will be fine.

It can work exactly the same with a wedding wish list in a shop. Select items from all ranges of prices so you cover people who can afford more expensive items and people who don't. This way, you can still have what you need for your home without having to ask directly for it.

When you send the wedding invites for example, you can add at the bottom or on back a link to the money pool or to your wedding list and a nice note saying roughly:

'If you want to help us fund our honeymoon, please find the money pool we created here. Thank you for making our dream come true'.

'If you want to help us make our new house a home, please find the wish list we created in XX shop here. Thank you for making our dream come true'.

38. After the wedding

After the wedding and your honeymoon if you plan to have one, sell everything you can. You can keep a couple of things as a souvenir but let's be honest, you are never going to use or look at them again. If you made your own decor, table centre pieces or if you have gift baskets, you can have at least a bit of your investment back, so sell as soon as you can. If you are planning to sell your wedding dress, shoes, suits, do it fast as clothes run out of style very quickly. If you wait for a year, they might not be trendy anymore and you might end up not selling at all, or for a very low price.

What is coming is not about saving money, but if you can afford it, then give everything away to people who can't or sell them at a very low price. My major job here is to make you save money, but sometimes it's nice to give back. So, unless you are very tight after your wedding or you need the money, make people happy with a selfless gesture. And sometimes, giving can come back to you in so many unexpected ways. So if you can, give it a shot!

39. It's time to talk about vouchers!

Whether you call them vouchers or coupons, it doesn't really matter. What we know is, it can help you save money. Do you enjoy going to the cinema, to the restaurants, to concerts, to the theatre or anything really? I am sure you can find one you will say yes to. Sooo, before buying a full price ticket for a new exhibition, check everywhere if you can find a promotion. It will take you 5 minutes of your time: just google 'voucher or promotion for xyz' and most of the time you'll find a discount. If you don't, well at least you tried. And truly, finding reductions, coupons or vouchers is not only for entertainment but for everything else. You can find amazing deals from just 10% off to 30% or more depending on if you are a first-time buyer or not. I can give you an example, I love eating at Pizza express and they had an offer of 2 for one on pizzas from Monday to Thursday. I discovered it by receiving Facebook ads and I saved the offer. Next time I went there, we saved almost half of the price of the bill when eating in for the 6 of us. I love the thrill of buying or eating what I want knowing that I saved money by using promocodes because I somehow think I am smart & I appreciate what I bought (tickets, food, clothes, furniture, anything really!) even more.

Spare your wallet by always looking online if you can find a better deal. I probably said it before and I say it again, but always do a little research before buying. We have the chance to be able to have millions of information at our fingertips, so use it!

40. For concerts, shows, plays, musicals, exhibitions, be open to not be on the 1st rows & think about seat filling, last minute ticket promotions and so on

I know, when going to a show, you want to be in the first few rows because well, they are the best seats, duh! Breaking news, you can still have a good time and see very well without being in the first few rows. This way, you can save money and enjoy the show. I love musicals and they tend to be expensive, so instead of buying an expensive ticket and seeing only one, I go a bit further and pay half the price (if not less!) and enjoy the same way I would have in the first row. Yes it is not as good, but shows are in places made to give you a good view, no matter where you are (except for seats with restricted views which I highly recommend to avoid). And for the price of one, you can end up doing 3 or 4.

For long running shows like plays, musicals and so on, I recommend you take a ticket during the week. They tend to be cheaper as less people can/want to go out during the week, especially on Mondays! Best is to book between Monday and Wednesday. This is not valid for all shows as some are very successful, and they can be fully booked all the time. But it is always worth looking if you can to save money. There is no harm in trying!

Last but not least, for entertainment, you have plenty of apps and websites to buy tickets at a discounted rate. You even have websites that offer you to fill seats for a very very small fee. I saw several plays for no more than £5 and it gave me the opportunity to discover plays I would have never thought about going to if I had to pay full price. When you pay full price, you want to be sure to enjoy the show as you paid a lot of money. But if it's dirt cheap, you can risk it and have lovely surprises. Seat filling is an amazing way to access culture for a very low price. But it isn't available for everything. So, when it isn't, you can always look at last minute ticket websites and apps that offer promotions. I love the app called TodayTix as they have regular promotions on a lot of different shows and if you turn on notifications on the app, you don't even have to look, they will send you messages to inform you of their best discounts when they are on. It is probably not the only one, but they used to have a referral program where you could get £10 off each time you refer to someone (and if I remember correctly, your friend gets the same). So discounted prices plus referral programs can make a good combo.

A quick Google depending on what you are after can save you a lot of money on shows. You might have different apps/websites depending on what you're after, so the best is to check online and sign up to their newsletter and apps. I wish you a good hunt!

41. Gym, are you really going to the gym?

We all dream to have the perfect beach body all year long. Some of us make it happen by going to the gym ... and some of us just buy a gym membership and don't go! Well, if you are from the first crowd then good for you, it's good for mental health. If you are from the second, then maybe it is time to stop the membership and save money! It's nice to have the will to go to the gym, but if you don't have the motivation, drop it. \Going to the gym is not for everyone, so if you want to practise a sport, explore before committing to yearly memberships.

If you haven't been to the gym before and you don't know if it's for you, try gym clubs that don't have yearly contracts and better if you can find one with no contracts at all. You can resign whenever and if you don't like it, then you would waste only a month of membership instead of a year. Other gyms offer a 3-month contract so it could be an alternative if you don't find one without a contract. I know it's more expensive per month, but let's be honest, if you don't like or don't go, it's better to lose 3 months of a more expensive price per month than 12 cheaper months. Keep that in mind when looking for a gym to go to.

And last but not least, if you go regularly to the gym, can you find a cheaper alternative? Depending on the equipment you need, have a look around and see if you can find a cheaper alternative. It takes 5 mins to Google and most gyms offer a free trial or daily pass so why not try? If you find that yours is a better value for the price, then stay & if you don't, you know what to do!

42. Let's talk babies & kids' clothes

Are you going to have your first child or do you already have kids? I talk about the first child as usually, parents spend a lot of money on clothes for the first one. Then they learn their lessons and whether it's recycling clothes from the first one or buying less expensive ones. We all want what's best for our children, but bear in mind, clothes for babies & kids don't last long. Sometimes you have to change them every two months, so why spend too much on something that your child isn't gonna wear for long or not have time to wear at all?

If your child isn't born yet, remember a lot of people will gift you new-born and baby clothes. Also, don't go crazy buying tons of clothes thinking they are gonna wear them because they mostly don't (except for pyjamas and bodysuits, you will need tons of them). Maybe you could make a list of what you need and let people participate instead of buying you random gifts.

Second solution is to buy second hand clothes. If you look online, you can find really cheap second hand clothes for kids and some of them can even be brand new for much less than in shops. These will come from parents who forgot they bought something or from a gift they forgot somewhere till it was too late. We all want new and shiny clothes, but keep that for when they get older and will enjoy it.

If you don't want second hand clothes, then you can just go buy new in shops like Primark or wait for the sales in Zara, h&m and other brands. They usually do good sales so you can save a lot.

So unless you can afford them, but again you wouldn't be here if you weren't trying to save money, it is not worth it to spend too much on kids clothes. And if you can afford it, then buy cheap and save the money into trusts for them to enjoy later. Trust me, you will thank me later.

43. ... And this is valid for all baby / grown up items

From the pushchair to the bouncer, you can find everything in the second-hand market. And sometimes, you can save up to 90% off the retail price, especially for baby items. After they are done with them, people will sell them very cheap to get rid of them, so this is your chance! So before buying brand new, have a quick look online, there are plenty of websites and apps where you can find what you are after. All you will need is a little cleaning after and you're good to go.

It applies to grown up items as well. It could be clothes, shoes, electronics, beauty products, whatever you need, there is 99% of the time a second-hand market for it. I am tempted to say 100% but I won't as I don't know everything. And so you know, sometimes people sell brand new things or used once items at half the price to get rid of them. Plus, it's good for the environment as there is less waste and less to recycle/destroy. Whether it's on Facebook marketplace, craigslist, gumtree, eBay or anywhere, it doesn't matter as long as you have a look at all of them depending on your location. I would tell you to Google it but Google doesn't always give you the best options & it doesn't know what is on Facebook groups or marketplace. Google for sure and then look around all the websites famous in your country for second hand items. I prefer buying from people rather than businesses, but it largely depends on what I am after. If you are after a Rolex, be careful where you buy it from to avoid buying a £5 one for £5000. Same applies to all luxury items. You have great private authenticators that can guarantee you if the item is fake or not. The more expensive it is, the more careful you must be. But it's definitely possible to buy a lot of things second hand, expensive or not. You just have to be cautious.

For example, when you buy electronics, always try them before buying and for more than 5 minutes. I once bought a bread maker for cheap (way too cheap, £5) and when I tried it at the seller's place it was working. It's only when I arrived home and tried it on to make bread that I understood why it was so cheap. After an hour of making the dough, the fuses tripped. I thought it was a coincidence, so I tried the bread maker again and the same thing happened. Needless to say, it ended up in the bin and I learnt my lessons. Thankfully, it was cheap. Never buy without trying properly.

If you buy a phone, you can type the serial number in a website to find out if it's a real one. It takes 5 minutes and can save you a lot of money. If you don't buy face to face, be sure to be able to send back the item or have a way of claiming your money back (with PayPal for instance). Never trust people with their word unless they can prove it. If the seller starts being aggressive or doesn't want to give you more details then steer clear, it's probably a scam.

And don't forget that if it's too good to be true, it probably is. So to sum up how to buy safely second hand items:

- If possible, buy face to face so you can check and test the item. If you can't, then make sure you have buyer protection. If it is a business, check their returns policy, depending on the country, you must have the option to return a defective item, second hand or not.
- When buying with a third party like PayPal, just make sure it is really PayPal and not a fraudulent website. Best option is to connect straight away and not wait for an email. If you receive an email, check the email address. Fraudulent emails always have weird email addresses. Don't click on any link sent by the seller.
- If it looks like a scam, it probably is so stay away. Trust your guts.
- For cheap items, you can try apps like depop or vinted, but for expensive ones, avoid as it's too dangerous on both seller and buyer's side.
- For expensive items, always ask for authentication or proof of authenticity unless it's a professional reseller with a return policy and verifier reviews.
- If you are selling something expensive, don't go alone as you never know who you are facing. Stay in public places and ask for cash or instant bank transfer. If you choose the second option, never give the item until you see the money in your bank account.

It might look scary to buy second-hand items online. It isn't, I am keeping you safe and mostly when buying expensive items (even if no scam is too small). We have tons of ways to buy second-hand safely so please, use them & enjoy buying second hand like I do!

44. Declutter and sell your unused items

Calling all the hoarders here: do you have clothes you haven't worn in 5 years? Do you have clothes that your kids were wearing that no longer fit ? Do you still have these (impulsive or not) buys that stayed with their tags? Do you have shoes that you wore once to find out they didn't fit you or aren't as comfortable as you thought? Do you tend to keep useless things that are just catching dust in your house?

If your answer is yes to at least one of these questions above, please read carefully.

You know and I know that YOU ARE NEVER EVER GONNA USE THEM! Yes I said it. We all like to keep things we no longer (or never) needed with this excuse: I will need it one day. NO, YOU DON'T. If you haven't used it in the past 6 months, it is very unlikely that you are going to need it at all. So, get rid of it, make some space and make some money at the same time. It doesn't matter how you do, but just sell them if they still have value. Organise a garage sale, go to a car boot sale, sell online, there are tons of options.

If you have too much clothes, sell them in bundles. People love it and yeah you might not make a lot of money out of them, but it's still better than keeping them. For more expensive and/or new clothes, sell them separately in app/websites for half their price, they will be gone in a jiffy.

When you have time on your hands, or at least once a year, go around your house and sort out what you still use and what you haven't used in a long time. And for things you don't use at the minute, have a serious think about you using them in the (near) future. If you are 100% sure you are going to use them, keep them, if you don't, sell them. For expensive or sentimental value items & to avoid having seller's regrets just have a good think about selling before committing and you'll be fine.

It will be so good for you to declutter and to make a bit of money at the same time. You will have more space for your feng shui or to buy new useful items. And it's good for the environment to repurpose old stuff, so it's a win for you, a win for your buyer and a win for the planet. You can thank me later ...

45. Do you need 10 identical tops?

Yes, I know, when you buy clothes, they never look the same. But well, sometimes they do. How many black tops do you need in your life? 10? 20? 2? I'd say around one for each season, maybe even 2 for each. This is what you need. That plus the other pile of clothes you have will help you survive spring, summer, autumn and winter easily. What you bought in the past is in the past, but in the future, before buying a new top, trousers, shirt, dress, anything really, just ask yourself: Do I have something similar at home? The answer is probably yes. If the answer is yes then drop it. Human beings are attracted to the same things and style and taste rarely change with time.

If it's no, then keep thinking. With what am I going to wear it? If you have nothing to match it with, then next you will have to buy something to wear it with. Great, more (useless) expenses. Where and when am I going to wear it? If you can't find an answer to these questions, you should probably leave it in the shops. We all have clothes we see that are amazing but we can't wear them because:

A- Wearing it might be harder than you think

B- You liked it in the shop but you're an introvert so don't go partying

C- It's makes you feel overdressed or underdressed everytime you are wearing it

D- It looks amazing but it doesn't fit or suit you

E- You are allergic to change so you keep wearing the same 3 outfits over and over again

Been there, done that! I always imagine myself in an outfit but it's a different story when I have to wear it, so take your time to consider if you are actually gonna wear it. Next questions are: is it a good value for money? Is it worth it? Should I wait for the next sales? Can I afford it?

If your answer is you need it, you don't have a similar one, it's a good value for money and you can afford it, then buy it. If not, then think twice. You don't need 3 times the same outfit style, especially when you usually stick to a couple of outfits. Then you eventually get bored of them, so you buy more. It's an endless circle of buying and not using, so unless you declutter too much and you need new clothes, open your wardrobe and have a good time looking for a hidden treasure.

46. Be careful buying clothes online

It's tempting, you have so much choice and it's usually much cheaper than in shops. You can spend hours scrolling into the million pieces they have. Facebook ads got you good, targeting you with the style and brands you like. Yes, buuuuuuuuuuut, we are smarter than that, aren't we?

I am not against buying online and I am not telling you to not buy online, just be frugal when you do.

Point made before, question yourself if you need it, can afford it and if it's interesting. In a word, look at point 44. And apart from that, you have to consider a few more things:

Is the website reliable & trustworthy? if it's famous then no problem, but if you've never heard of this website, a quick google might help.

Is the quality good? The look on a website might be a bit misleading, so be sure to receive the same piece of clothes you ordered.

How much is the delivery? If it costs more than the thing you bought, it might not be as interesting.

What is the return policy? This is for me the biggest issue you can face with buying online. You usually have time to send the items back, but if the returns aren't free, you'll lose money in the end.

And one more thing you need to factor before buying online, we have the tendency to buy more. Why? because it is cheaper, there is much more choice than in shops, they are making suggestions based on your style,, the clothes look amazing on a model and there are always good promotions, vouchers and so on. A lot of retail brands create a fear of missing out on clothes, like the 'only 1 left', "low stock' or on offers to push you to buy. They also create an urgency to make you buy quicker. Some of them have countdowns, emails with only 24 hours left to enjoy 50% off, flash offers and other tricks to make sure you see their offers and you are going to buy very quickly to not miss it. Nothing wrong with that, just don't be tricked into buying a Cruella costume because it's the last one & it's 50% off for a limited time only.

47. Buying brands

If you only like buying brands, have you ever thought of buying from outlets? Yes they can be a bit far from home but a trip once in a while can save you hundreds, especially if you prefer buying proper brands. If you can't really travel, try to find shops where you could buy brands at a discounted price. It would be smaller and with less options, but it will still make you save money.

And if you want to save even more, you should go during the sales when you can find some real bargains. Try to find an outlet where there are a lot of shops and even high-end/luxury and regular brands if you like both. Make it into a day trip where you are going to buy for you and your family if you have one and enjoy a nice lunch there. They all have decent food options now to make you stay and spend as much as possible. Most outlets have many shopping options from furniture, clothes, to high tech, so make a list of what you 'need' and go there when you are ready to buy. Bear in mind it can be a hit or miss, I've been to outlets many times without buying a single thing and other times, I found really good bargains. I said it before and I will say again, just don't buy for the sake of buying, just buy what you really want or need.

To piggyback on what was said about buying in outlets during the sales, let's now talk about SALES. It is an amazing time to find bargains and it can happen several times a year depending on your country! So yes, it's nice to be able to buy things for cheaper but (there's always a but) please organise yourself before going wild in the shops. How?

First, see if you can buy what you want before at a better price. As weird as it sounds and it probably depends on your country, but the sales period isn't always the time to have the best bargains. I noticed before that shops were doing better deals during black Friday, the last few days before Christmas or in the middle of summer. There is no logic or certainty as it could have been shops doing extra promotions to maximise sales, reduce their stocks or for any other reasons, so don't take my word for it but just keep an eye out on prices a few weeks before the 'classic' sales.

Then, you can define a budget. How much are you willing to spend for one thing and in total? For example, I have price points in my head for everything. If it's more than the price I defined, then I don't buy it because I don't think it's worth more than this price. I don't have a budget for the entire sales period as I usually don't find much but if you really like buying during sales, then you should set up a budget to avoid spending too much.

The best thing to do next is to organise what you want to buy by category and set up a budget for each or all together. For example, if you need furniture, then you might want to buy them first. List all you 'need' by priority and see what you can get within your budget.

This way, you will avoid buying things you already have or don't 'need' because it's cheap or a good bargain. Don't fall for the 'oh it's cheap' or 'I might use it/ wear it later', if you have no immediate use for it, let it go! We can get easily tricked on buying things because they are cheap & that is probably why sales were created in the first place. When you think about it, why would brands sell at a cheaper price & take a hit on their profits? Because they need you to buy old stocks to make space for the new one and stocking costs money to companies. So they are better off if you buy them and get them out of their stocks, even if they sell it for cheaper. And this translates into making seasonal sales for us, but rest assured, they always make a profit. In a nutshell buy what you want, not what you might think you want or 'just in case' because it's cheap.

48. Set a monthly/yearly budget for clothes

Are you a clothes' lover? Or do you know you're weak when it comes to buying clothes and you'll never be able to resist the urge of buying the latest trend?

If not, then you can skip to the next part. If this is you, then you should read the next few lines!

Again, been there, done that. Fast fashion is here to stay and designed to make you buy more all the time. Trends will never stop changing so you'll need to find a way to step back from your fashionable desire & from social media. Remember, we don't all have the same budget, some get clothes for free to promote them or worse, buy them & wear them for pictures and refund them. We, normal people and non-influencers, wannabe influencers or non rich people can't compete with that. I love to buy clothes but I calmed down on buying because I bought many things that don't suit me and never wore them in the end so now I am trying to buy less but better. I didn't set up a budget as I just stopped buying like people stop smoking. Sometimes I have a little relapse but most of the time, I am good. If you can't stop, then set up a monthly or yearly budget based on your income and the most important part: STICK TO IT! I find it a little difficult to stick to a yearly one but each to their own. You could have a monthly, bi-monthly, quarterly budget, whatever suits you best. It will be difficult at times but when you will get used to it, then you'll manage your money and only buy the pieces you really want & need. Most importantly, you'll learn to appreciate what you buy as you know you are limited & will have to wait for the next one to come. Your apartment, your wardrobe, your partner, your dog & cats will thank you for the extra space and money.

49. Find the best mortgage/ Renegotiate your mortgage

When buying a house or an apartment or for any big project, most of us will have to finance it with a mortgage. It only means you will borrow money that you will have to repay in 15 to 30 years (rough estimate depending on how much you borrow/the country you're from and so on). It is a big engagement in life but it's unfortunately necessary. If you do so, be sure to know everything before signing a long term contract.

First, get familiar with the concept. As stupid as it may sound, mortgages are more complicated than we think. And usually, it's only when it's too late that we get that. They are different types of mortgages and I am not gonna go into too much detail as they depend on the country you are from. For instance in the UK, you have the following options: Buy-to-let mortgages, Capped-rate mortgages, Discount mortgages, Flexible mortgages, Guarantor mortgages, Help to Buy mortgages, Joint mortgages and Offset mortgages. Be sure to understand what they are so you can find the right fit for you.

Second, and if you have time, look at the market. Some years are better to apply for a mortgage than others. Check when it is the best time (in your own time frame) to apply to have minimal interests. & Check with different banks or brokers and negotiate based on what you've been offered. The more, the better. If you don't have time to wait for the best time to borrow money, then at least compare as many offers as you can to be able to have the best one.

Third, when you get the mortgage, you should know that nothing is set in stone. You can negotiate your mortgage as many times as you like and there is no law against it (depending on your country). It is not always worth it, but it's always good to have a look and decide if it's time to renegotiate. If the market is worse than when you got it, then sit tight, and if it's better, then give a quick call to your bank.

It takes a lot of research and patience but doing this can make you save thousands so it's all worth it. And later when you're an expert, pass on the knowledge.

50. Renting vs Buying

I know people always say renting is a waste of money as it goes into someone else's pocket. It is true in a way, you don't invest the money you use for your rent. But is it really that simple? If it was, I bet everyone would own their place. Buying is a great thing when you can afford it. A lot can't as you need money to borrow money, utter nonsense, isn't it? Well, banks take cautions when lending money as they want to be sure they will get it back with interest. So yes, you technically need money to borrow money. So unless you come from old money, you'll probably need to rent for a while to build up savings to get a mortgage.

Apart from that, affording a £800 rent doesn't mean you can afford to repay a £800 mortgage. It is the same amount, but when you own a place, remember that you pay everything from your own pocket. If you are in a building, you'll have to pay for service charges and all the building work. I give you an example, if the stairs need to be redone, it will be a lump sum that will be divided between all the owners. Same for a house, your boiler breaks, you'll need to replace it and it isn't cheap. I don't say you can't but just be careful to be able to survive and have money on the side for these unfortunate and pricey events. So if you are paying £800 as rent and can't afford to put more into housing, you'll need to downsize to not struggle.

Owning an apartment or a house is one of the signs of 'success' or how 'you made it' that's why renting has a bad rap. The social pressure can be real when it comes to buying. There is no shame in renting even if you were to rent a place for the rest of your life. Renting has its perks like buying. Don't rush to buy just because others around you did, or because your parents told you it's time to own a place or you feel like it's missing in your life. Buy when you can afford it, are ready and find your dream place. No one's gonna pay for your mortgage so decide in your own time. Or don't, don't let anyone tell you what to do. Not even me 😃.

51. Is your rent too expensive?

If you can't afford to buy for now, then rent in a smart way. If your rent is too expensive, you can't sit, wait and mostly waste your money. There are several things you can do to keep your rent as cheap as possible.

Be on the look around to see if you can get cheaper. Sounds basic but the laziness in us prevents us from doing so. Set up alerts and see what happens. You might have started renting when prices were up and now you might get something for cheaper. Stay alert and you could save a lot in a year.

If you can't find it cheaper around, maybe it's time for you to live a bit further. I know it's not fun but we are here to save money! Sometimes even 20 mins away from where you are can be a lot cheaper. So look around and keep an open mind.

Also, if you really want to save, maybe you could consider sharing your flat or renting a room temporarily to split the rent? It's not a long term solution (unless moving with a partner or so we hope lol) but it could help you spare a few quids.

Is renting your apartment on airbnb an option? (with your landlord's approval of course] Even a few days a month can make a big difference in your budget.

It could cover your utility bills or just go straight into your savings.

In a word, try to be creative with your apartment to save money!

And by the way, the last two last ones also work if you own your own place. Just an idea, just in case.

52. Buying a (new) car?

If it's your first car and you are a new driver, don't spend too much money on it. Insurance is expensive and it will be even more expensive if you are a newbie. And that's not all, you are still learning so there are high chances of you damaging the car. It might be just scratches, but still. If you buy a valuable car, you'll cry every time something happens. So buy a cheap one for a few years so you don't mind too much if you do.

If it's not your first car (or even if it is), do you want to buy a new one straight away from the car dealers or a second hand one?

I would never recommend buying a new one as cars depreciate very quickly (except for the collectable ones) . As soon as the car is out and licenced, it loses value. The value decreases between 15 and 35% of the price in the first year and up to 50% or more over three years.[1] I understand the bliss of buying it brand new, but is it worth it? Not to me, but it's up to you.

Now that we've dealt with buying (or not) a new car, let's talk about financing the said car. Do you have sav-

---

[1] (source: https://www.moneyhelper.org.uk/en/everyday-money/buying-and-running-a-car/car-depreciation-explained#:~:text=Depreciation%20is%20the%20difference%20between, or%20more%20over%20three%20years.)

ings? If yes, use them. If you want to save money, I highly recommend not taking out a loan or using your credit card to buy it. Buy what you can afford even if it's not your dream car. The goal of a car is to take you from point A to point B so don't overspend for it. And worse, don't finance it with a loan that is going to cost you more than the car itself with interest. When you want to save money, one of the secrets is to only buy what you can afford. I probably said it before and I will say it again, only spend money on what isn't gonna cost you more in the long run. Hopefully one day, you'll have enough money to buy your dream car, but for now, make the reasonable choice and try to find a good deal.

How to find a good deal?

Do your own research (I know, I am a broken record). Start by narrowing down your choices to one model or a few similar ones. Then look at the options, if you want to buy new or used and so on. When you are decided, if you buy new, always ask for a discount. We don't think it's always possible, but it is. The market is harder than before so they will offer you freebies and probably a good discount. Don't hesitate to go to a few different ones and compare the discount they gave you. You can also mention that you've been before to others and they offered you a discount. If you buy a used car, you can always ask for a discount too. Just be careful not to be scammed. Test the car and if you aren't a mechanic, make sure to go with someone who will notice potential issues.

53. Let's talk about insurance & other fun topics

Whether it is for your car, for your house or anything else, Insurance is important and usually pricey. If you are looking for one, make sure to compare all of them before committing. Check the options and settle for the best value for money. Ask your friends and family if they can add you in a family plan or if they can refer you on their own. Most companies have referral schemes nowadays so make sure to look around. Also, a few companies have intro offers, for instance the first 2 months for free so you can save up a bit. Make sure it covers your basic needs and don't go for the full package if you don't need to because the insurer will tell you to go for the most expensive one, so just be careful.

Compare insurance prices both on their website and on comparison websites. Prices and offers can differ a lot from one to the other so make sure to check everything before making your final selection.

Utility bills, like insurance, are unavoidable. So, how can you cut costs there? Well, you can look at the competition and see if you can find a cheaper provider. If you can, then switch to a new one. If you don't find any cheaper, then try to change your behaviour to use less energy or water. You can find online a few hacks like switching off all electrical equipment at night, less baths and more showers, using your washing machine off peak, lowering the heating when possible ... I don't know all of them but they are very easy to find. Go get them now!

Now let's talk about mobile phones & contracts. I am sorry for this one but I never understood how people can spend more than their rent on a phone. I understand the hype and for some brands (not all unfortunately!), you can keep it for a few years but let's be honest, as soon as they are going to release a new one, you probably are going to buy it. If you can spend £1200 on a phone that ultimately is going to decrease in value, then to me you are wasting your money. It's a bad investment, just like cars. If you have a 6 figure salary or more, then ok why not, but if you are on minimum wage or 'regular income', why spend so much for something that has no more value than making calls, sending messages and going on social media? Yes you can use your phone for work and read your emails, but guess what? Lower value phones do it as well. You could invest this money and it could bring you so much more than a phone. At the end of the day it's your decision but I really really advise you to not buy expensive mobile phones and save your money for something that is really worth it. Whether you buy it cash or with a contract, it's still the same price. Actually, it is more expensive with a contract. Beware of contracts that offer you pricey phones for free or for a low price. You will pay for the phone one way or another. And usually, you'll forget about the contract and you will keep paying a lot every month for a phone that is probably already outdated.

The solution for me is to buy a cheapish & good quality phone that will have good reviews. There is plenty of choice now apart from the classic Samsung or Iphone so look around. When you find an affordable one, take a contract without a phone and compare all the network providers. You can find very good deals for contracts without phones, sometimes as cheap as £20 for a lot of data & free calls/sms. If you still want a contract that comes with a phone, I then advise you to negotiate every time your term is at its end. Negotiating could save you a lot of money. For example, if the contract is ending after 24 months, then the 23rd month, look around for better contracts/payment plans. If you find a worthy one, then quit as soon as you are done. If you don't, then notify your provider you would like to end the contract and they will make you an offer. If you call them asking for a better deal, they will give you a little something. If you ask to resign, then they will offer you a very good deal to retain you. Good luck!

A little one that we spend so much on without thinking: Restaurant, takeaways and drinks. It's nice to go for drinks, eat at the restaurant or sometimes when you are lazy, order a takeaway. But don't do it too often if you want to save money, you need to keep it under control.

You're thinking, 'oh one drink won't hurt', but one drink at £6 3x times a week is £18. It's £72 a month minimum. And let's be honest, we rarely stop at one drink. I don't tell you to stop socialising but try to keep your drink spends at the minimum. It's really easy to spend a lot in a week without even noticing.

If you really like to go to restaurants, keep it as a treat. We all love to go to the restaurants but it's the same as drinks, even if you don't go to expensive ones, it can easily be a lot of money out the window in a month. Try to stick to one max per week and you should be fine.

Takeaways are nice and convenient but the more you are going to order takeaways, the more you'll be lazy to cook and choose the easy way out. It takes a few clicks as opposed to cooking so, don't go into this habit of ordering food all the time when you don't feel like cooking. You can do it sometimes, but with moderation. Everything is ok with moderation. Not more than once a week for instance. If you don't like cooking like me, try to look online for quick, easy and tasty recipes. You have so many options out there that take less than an hour & sometimes less than half an hour. And cook more than one meal at a time so you don't have to cook everyday. Cooking is cheaper than buying food from outside and it's better for you as well. Takeaways should be a treat from time to time, not your main food source.

54. Credit card and cash back

I won't lie, I am not a fan of credits and credit cards, but I think by now you kinda understood. It's a slippery slope as it's not money you have and you'll spend the rest of your life paying for it. This is how banks trick you, they give you a credit card, you use them to pay everything and before you know it, you owe them money for the rest of your life. So I will say, unless you need one for a specific project, steer clear. Keep your debit card to only spend the money you really have. I know in some countries you feel like you need one and it's a cultural thing, but trust me, coming from a country where it isn't the rule, you don't need one for your daily life. If they give you one when you apply for a mortgage, just keep it but don't use it. Maybe keep it in case of an emergency. But just don't use it, especially for unnecessary things. Use loans or mortgages for a business, for an emergency abroad, for a big project, for a house, for anything that will bring you something bigger in the future.

If you have one and want to use it, you might as well take advantage of it. Check all the coverage you can have when you use it and check the cashback options.

Even if cashback is more popular with credit cards, you can also find it with debit cards. With cashback, you can make a few hundreds a year when you use your card. Don't spend easily because they give you a few percent back. Always buy what you need and spend smartly while making a few quids back.

55. Be careful with small loans & instalment payments

Small loans can be handy & usually, companies don't ask for too much before giving you the money. Have you asked yourself why? Because the interest rate is usually a lot higher than 'regular banks'. The companies offering these loans target people who are desperate for money and need it quickly. Or worse, people who don't know how to manage their money and end up in debt. Some people live above their means and spend like there is no tomorrow when in fact, there is! Bitch you might still have 40 years to live.

And who is in this situation? Not wealthy people of course and not people with a lot of savings or stable financial situation. It will cost you so much more than saving and buying it in cash. If you really need one and if you have no other choice, then do it but I highly recommend you to avoid it at all cost. A lot of people end up in a really bad financial situation because of this. It's a vicious circle. You take it because you need the money then end up more in debts because you can't pay for this. People usually take them when they are not financially stable or don't have enough savings and need a wad of cash. You take a loan because you really need it fast. It's quick & easy to get so it's great. Then comes the time you need to give the money back with interest and you realise how high they are. If you don't have a lot of savings or a lot of money, once you are done with paying the basics in your life, you will be very quickly overwhelmed. So, I'd recommend steering clear of these small loans from credit companies that only need your name, full address and number to give you a credit card or money.

Same goes for instalment for items. Remember, companies offering you to pay for a 4k TV in 10 payments aren't doing it as a favour to you but for money. They are businesses and their aim is to make money. If you really need to buy something that you can't afford to pay, it could be a solution, but first please calculate the total amount it's going to cost you before committing to it. And only use these types of payments for 'real' necessities like a washing machine or anything you absolutely need and not just the latest fancy TV or a bunch of clothes from a website. it's so easy to pay in instalments and before you know it, you could have a few hundreds out of your bank account every month because you thought it would be ok as it's not a small amount. Paying in instalments gives you the false impression of not paying as much as if you were paying for an item at once. Because it's £100 for 15 months (Plus interest) instead of £1500 at once, you are like it's just a hundred. Except it isn't! It will cost you more in the long run because of the interests. Pay upfront and you will think twice before buying something expensive.

You can use instalments if you really need something but remember to keep it under control and avoid reaching out to it as much as possible. It is still better than small loans but it's still not a good thing. You pay more than the real price and you will be more tempted to use it all the time. More and more companies are offering these options, so be careful how and when you use it.

56. In need of money quickly?

Why not take a second job if you can? I am not telling you to ruin your health by working two jobs for the rest of your life but if you need money for a big project, why not take a second job for a limited period of time to save as much money as possible. Before I bought my apartment, I had a Monday to Friday job and a Saturday morning job at the market. It was just 7 more hours but it helped me save my monthly salary as it could cover my weekly groceries for instance or anything else. Don't be afraid to sacrifice a bit of your life to achieve your goals. It isn't ideal and the ideal would be that we would all have high paying jobs, but this is reality. If you aren't born into money, you are going to have to make sacrifices to make money. It could be taking a second or third job, creating your company while working full time, anything really. Saving money might be the push you will need to achieve your goals but sometimes, you don't have that much cash left at the end of the month to save, so you'll need to find a way to make that extra cash. You can be the smartest and yet don't make ends meet if you don't manage your money correctly. Success comes from 90% of hard work and 10% of talent. Some people make it just with their hard word and smart ideas, no real talent. But the main factor is hard work, so maybe you can sacrifice a bit of your time for now to be successful in the future. Believe in yourself, work hard and spend wisely. When you have the cash then invest it and hopefully one day, all that hard work will pay off. Nothing bad comes from working hard and being money savvy.

Also, if you are in between jobs for any reason and struggle to find a new one, don't be afraid to take a lower paid job or contracts till you find your perfect fit. It could take weeks or months before you do, so in the meantime don't drain your savings waiting for the job. Take an easy to leave job that can cover your basic necessities and allow you to look for another job or work on your personal projects. Savings melt as fast as ice in the sun so keep them for big projects or emergencies, you never know when you are going to need them. And you never know where great opportunities lie.

57. My sleep on it rule

I have a rule whenever I want or need to spend a lot of money at once. I wait till the next day or even leave it for a few days. It is not so much when I need something because well, I'll have to buy it anyway, but more on when I really want something that is pricey, not always worth the money but I want to treat myself. Let's say you fancy buying yourself a new car and the car you always wanted was a Mercedes. You have the money to buy it, but do you really need it? Obviously not. Do you want it? Obviously, yes. For a big buy like that, you need to think, can I really afford it in the long run? Buying it is one thing, but insurance is going to be more expensive, petrol as well, MOT and any other expenses are going to be more expensive than a toyota. But apart from that, you need to think, is it worth it? and mostly, is it worth putting that money I could save in a car? Or is it worth sacrificing my savings for this car? Some will say yes, others will say no, each to their own. What I am trying to say is, as soon as you need to spend a lot of money, sleep on it. Leave it 24 hours, a few days, a few weeks and even a few months. If you still want it real bad, then buy it because it might make you feel good. If after a few days you are doubting yourself or you almost forget about it, then don't. If you could forget it easily, it won't bring you any satisfaction or not what you expect from it.

So remember, sleep on it, when the excitement is gone, you'll be able to make the best decision. Don't impulse buy pricey things, unless you can refund them easily (but still don't!).

58. Always plan your holidays a LOT in advance (unless you absolutely can't)

No secret or rocket science here, the more you plan in advance, the cheaper holidays will be. Apart from the odd chances of having a last minute cheap plane ticket, the sooner the better. You will have more options in terms of flights, accommodations and will have more time to compare offers and choose the cheapest option or at least the best value for money. I am more of a last minute holiday planner, so trust me I know. I tend to not know in advance when and where I am gonna travel so I just end up taking what is left or spend hours a day trying to find the best value for money. As you may have understood by now, I like to save and to spend as little as possible so I will search every possible way to find the best value for money.

The closer you get to the date, the less you have options, so when I can, I try to plan 3 months in advance. This way, the holidays don't feel too far away and I get to have more options. But ideally, planning a year in advance or between 6 months and a year is the best. Train, plane or bus tickets are cheaper and you'll have all the accommodations still available. If you have kids, it's even more important that you plan ahead. You always know when you can and can't go on holidays.

The dates are always set so out of all the school holidays you have, just decide in which one you will travel and in which one you won't. Travelling during half term is 3 times more expensive than during the rest of the year so the sooner you plan, the more you can save money. You could maybe use it during your holidays, or to save for the next one. Prepare your bucket list and be on the lookout 👀.

59. Search thoroughly for travelling tickets ...

Be your own Google! If you want to go to a country, always compare prices. What prices? First, you will check if it's better to take a package holiday or book everything separately. Most of the time, the second option is cheaper for the same holidays (and sometimes a looooot cheaper), but it's not always true so the best solution is to compare both. It's super easy, you just go online, look at the cheapest package holiday on different websites for the selected destination and have a look at the flight tickets only for the same dates. If the first option is cheaper, it's because they have special flights that allow them to have very competitive fares. If it is the case, then book the package holiday with confidence. If the second option is cheaper, then you will have to do a bit more work to find the best bargain. But at the end of the day, you could save 1/3 of the price or maybe more. Trust me, it's so worth it. As an example, I spent 12 days in Mauritius for the price of 7 days by comparing the two.

For option two, the hunt starts now. Choose if it's better to take your car (if it's even possible), a train, a coach/bus or a flight. For the coach, bus or plane tickets, check all the companies and which one is the cheapest.

If you are on a budget, taking coaches might be your best option so don't rule it out too quickly. It's not the fastest option for sure, but it is the cheapest, so it can help you travel on a budget. Trains can be pricey, it depends where you want to go. I suggest checking the prices first and comparing them with flights. Flights can be the cheapest as well. To give you an example, flights are cheaper from London to Paris than taking the 2 hour train, especially if you book your ticket at the last minute. In that instance, trains might be 3 times or more expensive than a flight. For long flights, check if it's cheaper to have a stopover somewhere. If you can save a lot and the stopover is not more than 3 hours (for a long flight), you might want to book the cheapest option. If it's not a massive difference, it's better to take the direct flight. Time is money too! For short flights, I only recommend direct flights. You usually don't save that much and it will lengthen your journey for next to nothing. Now that you booked your travel ticket, let's see how you can save on accommodation.

60. ... Accommodation

Accommodation can be more expensive than the flights at times so you better be prepared. Look at all the options: hotels, bed & breakfasts, apartments or rooms with airbnb or any other website and choose which option is the best depending on your plan. Because, yes, you need to plan your trip first! Are you planning to stay in more than one place? Are you renting a car? It will determine how far you can be from the centre or from where you want to go and you might allow yourself to go a bit further to have a better place to stay for cheaper. Do you want any facilities? Do you want full board, half board or just breakfast? If there is no meal included, are there enough restaurants or supermarkets around? When you are done with the planning, then you can start with the booking. I won't tell you to book a cheap accommodation, I am telling you to find the best price you can. How? By comparing the websites. Booking, airbnb, hotels.com, agoda, you name it. Just check all of them, you might see a huge (or small) price difference between them. Also, check if you can find voucher code to use on the websites. Even a 10% discount is still better than nothing. 10% of £700 is £70 and it all adds up. Once you find the cheapest option, just book it! And just a kind reminder: do not spend money you don't have, saving is possible in holidays too.

One more, once you find the place you want, google again to check if it has its own website. If they do compare between booking platforms and their own. It can be cheaper but it's not always the case. Sometimes reservation platforms are cheaper than the accommodation website. Plus, you can have online discounts (like secret prices in hotels.com or genius with booking) or discount codes to make it even cheaper. Before booking anything, always check if you can have some sort of discount.

If you are already in the country, you can always ask for a discount to the hotel directly based on what you are seeing online. It happened to me before and most would rather give you a discount and take the full amount than paying fees to the reservation platforms. It is a good solution especially if you are looking for a last minute accommodation.

61. ... And the rest

Once the mains are booked, you can look at the rest in more detail. Is it cheaper to rent a car or to travel with local buses/trains/rides? If it's easy , safe and cheap, choose local transport. If it's tricky, rent a car. When you rent a car, just don't take the first option you find. When you book your flight, check if the rental price offer is worth it. Before booking your rental car with your flight, compare it to a few other car rentals, especially local ones. If option 1 is cheaper, book your car with your flight, if it's not, you already know the answer. If you are going to use a car during your entire trip, I recommend you book one before arriving, one you can find at the airport or where you arrive. It will save you the cost of travelling to your hotel and you won't waste time looking for a car rental there.

Is it cheaper to book visits online before or is it cheaper there? You might go on social media and blogs and try to gather as much information as you can before. People usually have tons of tips that might help you make the best of your trip & save at the same time. Remember, buying locally is always cheaper, even in Japan.

I might be hated for that one but sorry, hotel tours are the most expensive (99% of the time). I travelled a fair bit and tours being cheaper at the hotel only happened to me once. If you are lucky, there isn't a big difference, but most of the time, you can save around 30% at least. So what I suggest is to wander around and check tour prices to compare with the hotel prices first. So you know, they are all the same tours, they are just taking different commissions. So have a little look around and remember, you can always negotiate the prices of tours or at least try. Most of them, hotels included, always have room for a little negotiation so channel your inner negotiation king.

62. Do you want to travel but you don't know where or you are on a budget? No problemo

There is a magical box in skyscanner you can tick if you don't know where you want to go. Whether you are on a budget or looking for inspiration, this little box might be for you. It gives you a price range for all the destinations by continent and countries. The more specific you are with your dates, the more prices are accurate. It also gives you a price range for accommodations but it's usually for hotels only so if you want to rent a room or an apartment, the price might differ. Once you narrow down where you want to go, you can always have a look at other websites to compare the fares. If you are on a budget, you might want to look at the accommodation first before booking your flights. Earlier, I said that for some destinations, flights are the cheapest so you don't want to end up over budget because you didn't check first. I think it's great to have an idea of the price first and plenty of choices and you can pick based on your budget. You might not have thought about going to this destination before but hey, I am sure you will find plenty of options that are on your bucket list. My bucket list isn't set in stones, so maybe yours isn't too?

If you are flexible with your travel dates, you can also check the prices for a month or several months for a destination and book the cheapest ticket within this time frame. You can do the same for package holidays, prices are more expensive if you fly on a weekend or at specific dates for various reasons.

A little advice though, before booking a trip, always check if it is the right season to go visit the country. You don't want to end up in a week of rain, typhoon or hurricane during your holidays.

63. How to exchange money at the best price when you travel (...or not)?

First, you can start by monitoring the exchange rate online. It will give you an idea of how much you are going to get for your money. Then, check what is the best method to pay in the country: card or cash. Remember, in a few countries, cards are not used a lot or non-existent so you will need a lot of cash. Then, you can ask on social media groups or pages where people usually exchange money in the country you are going to travel to.

Sometimes it's better to exchange money in your own country before leaving, sometimes it's better there at the airport or in town. I usually found that exchanging money at the airport isn't the best option, but again it depends on the country. Plus, you'll find countries that don't have a lot of money exchange offices so you might struggle to exchange money. Just check all the options you have and if it's easy to access money too. It doesn't matter how you access money, ATMs or cards but you need to know if it's easy in case you need to.

The touristy places have a lot of money exchange offices so check a few of them before exchanging money. General rule too, if there is more than one, always check as much as you can before exchanging money. Ask for the rate (if not clearly written) and the fees you might have. Some places will give you a better rate if you exchange more money. You can always try to negotiate the rate but it doesn't work everywhere. Bear in mind that the rate you are getting is never the forex one as it's the one used by financial institutions. But try to get as close as possible. Also, unless you are staying for a long time or don't have an easy way to exchange money, try to change your money little by little as you go. It will be much easier than coming back with it or exchanging it back and losing money in the process.

If you can and prefer to pay by card, check what the fees are and so on before leaving. If you have a card like Wise, Monzo or Revolut, you might have a better rate than with a classic card from a 'classic bank' and most likely no or very little fees. Classic banks offer no fees on certain destinations but the rate is not great unless you have a very specific (and expensive) card made for it. Whatever you do, check first as the fees and exchange rates quickly end up as a bad surprise on your bank statements. Paying by card might be better if you play your cards right. For example, I found it cheaper in Turkey to pay my Revolut card than exchanging money in the offices. It doesn't matter how many I checked, paying by card was always much better.

Last but not least, and this one is just to keep in mind, why not use remittance websites to send yourself money at the best rate? They sometimes have the best rates so why not check Western Union, WorldRemit, Remitly, Moneygram and co? You can send yourself money and pick it up in minutes depending on the website/app and destination. Just remember you need to have cash pick-up available and that you can really pick it up where you are before sending money to yourself. And if you want to send money abroad, it works the same way. We have many options now to have a good rate and lower fees so why not take advantage of them.

64. Found something cheaper abroad? Bring it with you!

I know it can sound weird, but if I find something I use or like abroad, I'll buy it and bring it back with me. I bought toothpastes, cheap coconut hair oil, a very cheap teapot and glasses from Dubai and many other gems from different countries. It can be anything as long as it fits in my suitcase and it's not illegal to travel with. Again, you have to make sure it's worth it and you will use it. If it's just to save 10p, it's definitely not worth the effort. Or if it's just an impulse buy, you might regret it later.

Some brands are cheaper in their native country or adapt to their markets. Zara is a good example of price differences between countries: it is cheaper in Spain and Portugal compared to the rest of Europe and it's even more expensive in the US and UAE. Prices will obviously vary depending on the shipping costs, taxes and whatnots within the country, but if you fly from New York to Barcelona, you might want to wait to buy from the Spanish brands. You might save a lot, especially if you go there during the sales. Same goes for Apple. It is cheaper in the US compared to France for example and even more expensive in the UK. Electronics can be cheaper in Asian countries too, so you might want to check if you are planning to travel and want to buy something specific. Just a quick search will give you an answer and will save you money (or avoid spending more!).

And if you buy abroad, remember to claim the taxes back before you leave the country. It is very easy now and it can be done in a couple of minutes. Depending on the country, it can be a lump sum so it's worth looking into it. Ask the shops where you intend to buy how to proceed, I am sure they will be happy to help. Some even offer detax in the shop directly so don't forget your passport when shopping!

65. Sell in preparation for the Christmas shopping

How many times a year do you go through your things and sell what isn't used? Once a year? Twice? Never? Well you should do it at least twice a year I'd say, but do it in preparation of Christmas especially if you are short on money. We all have clothes, toys, electronics we don't use so why not sell them to have spare cash to spend on Christmas? You have many many apps, websites and car boot sales nowadays where you can sell your used stuff to make money. You won't make a lot of money out of second hand items apart from the very sought after ones. Who knows, maybe you'll find a treasure you will sell 10 times the price you paid for it. Look at people with pokemon cards, who knew some of them would be worth the price they are today? It doesn't happen to everything so let's be realistic here. But you can sell pretty much everything as long as it's in good condition. If you have unworn clothes or toys and you know for sure they aren't going to be used, take a few pictures and start selling. Declutter, sell and set the money aside for your Christmas money. Your wallet and your home will thank you for it! Giving a second home to your items will make everyone happy: you by getting money, the buyer for buying it cheaper (not everyone can afford to buy new or simply don't want to buy new) and the planet as it's not going to end up in landfill or in the ocean. It's a win-win for everyone.

66. Buy your gifts in advance

Christmas is every year on the same day, isn't it? So why wait until the last minute to start buying gifts? Even November might be too late. I know it's not always easy to plan in advance for kids as they might want the last trendy gift, but for the most part (and even for kids), you might be able to buy the gifts a lot in advance. Write what you need to buy in a list and start looking at the prices around. If you have enough time before Christmas, you might be able to monitor the prices for a bit and find yourself a promotion to buy it at a discounted price. It obviously depends on what you want to buy but as said before, you can always find a voucher code or there will be times when the brand you are after is having small or big sales. So, why pay full price at the last minute (and sometimes finding it sold out) when you can buy it for cheaper? Key to saving money is to plan in advance for everything so you have time to find the best price. Be organised for everything, especially for events like Christmas as it can be overwhelming and it involves spending a lot of money. You spend money for gifts, for a Christmas tree, for decorations, for food, maybe for new clothes and so on. So save where you can by organising your gift purchases in advance. It takes very little plan for probably big savings. This works for all events like birthdays, Eid, Hanukkah, Mother's and Father's day and any other day that requires a gift.

67. Not looking for a specific gift?

Not everyone can afford to buy specific gifts or not everyone has a list for Christmas. This is when you have to be creative. How? First off, as said above, look at all the websites, apps, car boot sales where you can find gems and a bargain at the same time. A lot of people (me included in the past) impulse buy clothes among other unnecessary items. It was a good idea on the spot but it was kept unused. So I, like other people, try to sell these online. And, this is where you go into action. You know your spouse wants a Bose headphone, try to buy it from someone who is selling it before buying it from the shops. On a side note, be careful with counterfeits, warranty and all that. You will find a lot of brand new clothes and toys. People usually give a lot of clothes and toys kids aren't gonna use because their parents simply forgot about them or they weren't at the right size for the right season. So especially for kids, you will want to look on second hand websites before buying from the shops.

Also, if you aren't after something specific, just go to outlet shops and see if you can find a bargain. Shops like TKMAXX have plenty of good options for everyone but not only them, you can find outlet shops pretty much everywhere nowadays. Give it a go before buying at full price. I did it several times and it worked like a charm every time. Key is to know their tastes and you will find for sure something they like somewhere. Just Google if you have any around you or simply if you can buy from them online and have a blast. If you have a specific brand in mind and they don't have an outlet, check if they have a sale section in their website. Most do online.

In a nutshell, look around offline and online to find cheaper alternatives to what you want to buy. Again, it takes a bit of organisation as you will need time to look around and find the perfect gift. This also works for all types of events that have the same date every year.

68. Not planning to see your family on Christmas day?

I know it sounds weird, but not everyone is able to see their family on the D day. For many different reasons like living abroad, you have to see your partner's family and so on. If you are one of these people, then maybe you should wait for the sales (if they are after Christmas in your country) to buy your gifts. If you can wait, you might save 50% or more (or less) on gifts. There is no rush to buy them for the specific date so give it a go and see how it works. Though there are sales all year now with Black Friday that is not only in the US nowadays, Cyber Monday and many other sales around November, you might still want to wait for the 'real' sales to find the real bargains. I guess it's just about looking at the prices during all of the sales before and if you find a decent price, then just buy it. I found Black Friday pretty useless in France as the discounts aren't great but it must be different in other countries. I heard in the US it's pretty good but again, if there is no rush you might want to wait to find the same prices with a smaller crowd. Some people are still ready for the sales but others are just skint. To me, if there is no rush, I'll wait til what I am after is on sale. If I have time, I just want to save as much as I can so I wait for the best until I can't wait any no longer.

69. Recycle your Christmas gifts

Whether they are from your birthday, Christmas or any other celebratory gift, we all had at least once gifts we didn't like. You have to pretend that you like it in front of the person. Smile and say thank you like you mean it. But let's be practical. You don't like it for a reason, so you most likely aren't going to use it. I have two options for this: option one is to gift it to someone else and option two is selling it.

    For option one, you just have to be sure that the person who gave it to you and the person you will give it to don't know each other and are never going to meet. You don't want to be rude by openly showing you don't like their gift, do you? Good! When you are sure that they can't connect the dots, you save your money by not having to buy a gift and you (potentially) make someone happy. This way, it doesn't sit in your home catching dust. It's not really nice but well, if you have no use for it, you might as well help it reach its potential in another home.

    For option two, we talked about it earlier when buying, and guess what? Now, you are the seller of unwanted gifts. Take nice pictures and put it in all the websites/apps where you can sell second hand items. Be prepared to not have the full price of the item back but that's the game, people are after a bargain and you want to make something of this unused item that will only be dusting your home. Do a price check online and find out if it's a sought after and sold out item. If it is, you might even make more than what it was really worth. When the price check is done, just think of the lowest price you want to take for it. Then add a few pounds to leave room for negotiation because most people will negotiate. It doesn't matter how cheap you are selling it, they will try to have it for cheaper. If something is worth £100 and you are selling it for £50, you might have people offering you £25, true story. It happened to me several times before. So just from personal experience, never put the price you have in mind but put a higher price so people can feel like they negotiated well and got a bargain while you sold it at the price you wanted all along!

Conclusion

I guess saving money is about keeping your spendings under control & track where you can save to avoid wasting money. But it's not the only thing. It's about being organised and thorough. It's about not succumbing to spending money on everything 'you think you deserve, or to treat yourself' and living from paycheck to paycheck. It's about not comparing yourself to others and wanting the same expensive car, watch, clothes, trips, anything you can't afford at the time. It's about stepping back from all the fake social media lives you see & from the TV programmes selling you a luxurious lifestyle. It's about you realising we are not born with the same chances in life but we can to some extent change our future. Marginal gains can have a massive impact on your life too. It's about you planning ahead and thinking long term solutions rather than little short term fixes.

 The biggest advice I can give you would be: don't let things possess you. No clothes, cars, apartments, nothing is going to make you feel happy and fill the void you may have. It is just an instant pleasure that you'll need to repeat in order to feel good again, just like drugs. It's a never ending process. Buy what makes you happy but don't plan on buying to feel happy.

You can always start small and remember, it's never too early or too late to start!

If you are bad at saving money, start small and go bigger. Try to buy coffee outside 3 times a week instead of 5, then food outside 4 times instead of 5, then little by little, you will get used to saving money. The more you will save money, the more you will want to save. If you are a student and you can save, start already. If you can't because your expenses are too much, then start later when you can. If you spent most of your adult life not saving and you think it's too late to start, it isn't. It's never too late for anything, but especially this. It doesn't matter if you are 20 or 70, you can do it. Of course, it's better and easier to try when you're young(er) but, well we all have different backgrounds, different lives, different goals in life. We change, we evolve, we fail and start again. I was myself not very good at savings, I was travelling a lot and throwing money a lot. Then one day, I decided it was time to change. Why? Because I realised, I wanted more than instant 'happiness fixes' from buying things I didn't need. I saw my wardrobe full of unused clothes that I will never wear. I got tired of drinking and eating outside. I started saving money and I liked seeing the money in my bank account going up and up so I wanted to save even more. There are still months where I spend most or all of my salary because I am still travelling and enjoying my life, but if I do, then when I come back, I try to live as frugally as possible. Life is about balance and you should treat your money/expenses the same way. I spent a lot this month for xyz reasons, the next month or the following months, I'll keep my spendings to the minimum.

I hope these few simple tricks will help you save at least a few pounds a month and before you know it, you'll have a lump sum to your name.

www.ingramcontent.com/pod-product-compliance
Lightning Source LLC
Chambersburg PA
CBHW052208220526
45471CB00004B/1870